step-by-step

Polymer Clay

IN A DAY

step-by-step

Polymer Clay

IN A DAY

Over **15** exciting projects, from gifts to accessories for the home

EMMA RALPH

NORTH LIGHT BOOKS

CINCINNATI, OHIO
www.artistsnetwork.com

Dedication

With love to Leslie, Mum, Dad and Dorian. Thank you for the
support and encouragement you have each given me in so many ways.

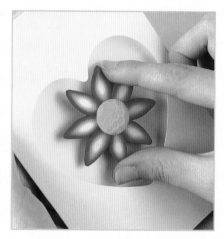

First published in 2004 by New Holland Publishers (UK) Ltd
London • Cape Town • Sydney • Auckland

Garfield House, 86–88 Edgware Road, London W2 2EA, United Kingdom
www.newhollandpublishers.com

80 McKenzie Street, Cape Town, 8001, South Africa

Level 1, Unit 4, 14 Aquatic Drive, Frenchs Forest, NSW 2086, Australia

218 Lake Road, Northcote, Auckland, New Zealand

First published in North America by North Light Books, an imprint of
F + W Publications, 4700 East Galbraith Road, Cincinnati, Ohio 45236
Tel: 1-800-289-0963

ISBN 1-58180-491-1

Editorial Direction: Rosemary Wilkinson
Senior Editor: Clare Sayer
Photographer: Shona Wood
Design: Glyn Bridgewater
Production: Hazel Kirkman

Reproduction by Pica Digital PTE Ltd, Singapore
Printed and bound in Malaysia by Times Offset (M) Sdn. Bhd.

Note

The information in this book is true and complete to the best of our knowledge. All
recommendations are made without guarantee on the part of the authors and the
publishers. The authors and publishers disclaim any liability for damages or injury
resulting from the use of this information.

Acknowledgements

Many thanks to Staedtler (UK) Ltd, especially Kathryn and Rieka, for providing the
Fimo polymer clays and Easy Metal used in the book and for never saying "No"
when I asked for more! My thanks also to all the other companies who gave their
time and support, especially Jane Giles at Craft Creations Ltd., Doug Friedman at
Polyform Products Co. and Corrine Hildreth of Rupert, Gibbon and Spider Inc.
Thanks also to everyone at New Holland (UK) Ltd for bringing everything together
so beautifully, to my mum for feeding us all and to my friends and fellow polymer
clay artists who have been so wonderfully supportive.

Contents

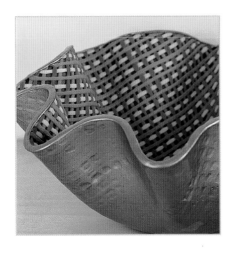

Introduction

Polymer clay is fun stuff! If you have not already fallen in love with this amazing home-bake clay, then believe me – you soon will! Polymer clay is a colorful, pliable modelling material that is very easy to use. You can mold it and texture it, sculpt it and fold it, even use it to mimic other materials such as stone, glass or metal. It is available in many vivid colors and speciality formulations, from stone effect to glow-in-the-dark, plus translucent and even liquid clays too. All of which offer unlimited creative potential for making jewelery, sculptures, miniatures, mosaics, bowls, boxes and many other items. By simply rolling, cutting and shaping the clay, you can easily master an array of highly decorative techniques, whatever your artistic abilities.

Although I refer to it as clay, this material is not actually a "clay" in the traditional sense. Polymer clay is made synthetically from Polyvinyl Chloride (PVC) particles mixed together with plasticizers and pigments. The PVC particles fuse together when heated to form a durable plastic. It only needs the low temperatures provided by your kitchen oven, not the costly high-firing kilns that ceramic clays require. So, unlike other crafts, you will not need a lot of expensive equipment to use polymer clay. Your kitchen oven, some basic tools and a block of clay will be more than enough to start you on your way.

In *Step-by-Step Polymer Clay in a Day* I have concentrated on making gifts, home accessories and jewelery in 12 simple-to-follow projects – all of which can easily be completed in under a day. In the projects, I quantify the clays needed in terms of "blocks". Most brands of polymer clay are sold in small blocks of around 60 g (2 oz) and a block in the project refers to this amount.

For simplicity's sake, I also refer to scrap clay in the same way. It is far easier for you to judge the volume by eye than having to weigh out different amounts.

If you are already a dedicated "clayer", I hope you will enjoy these projects and the new approaches they offer. But for those of you who are new to polymer clay, fear not! The opening chapters will provide you with a solid foundation, teaching you the key skills used in the projects and much more besides. The projects can all be adapted, so experiment with other techniques and variations, adding your own personal touches here and there.

I also hope that this book will encourage you to explore polymer clay further, beyond the scope of these pages. With the growth in internet use, a strong on-line community has developed, with polymer clay artists sharing ideas and building friendships. So, there are plenty of web pages and discussion groups for you to check out, and a very friendly bunch of clayers just waiting to meet you! There are also many polymer clay guilds now all around the world – there may well be one near you. Why not get in touch to enjoy regular meetings, lessons and weekend retreats?

It has been over 15 years now since I bought my first packet of polymer clay. I still remember the very first pin I made and the delights of stumbling across new techniques as I experimented further. That fascination with this remarkable "clay" has never left me. I hope that polymer clay will fascinate you just as much, bringing you the excitement, friendship and creative satisfaction it has brought me.

Emma
Ralph.

About Polymer Clay

There are many different brands of polymer clay available for you to use. Essentially they all contain the same ingredients but the characteristics of each brand do vary. No one brand is best overall; when choosing clay, select the product with the best characteristics for the particular project in hand.

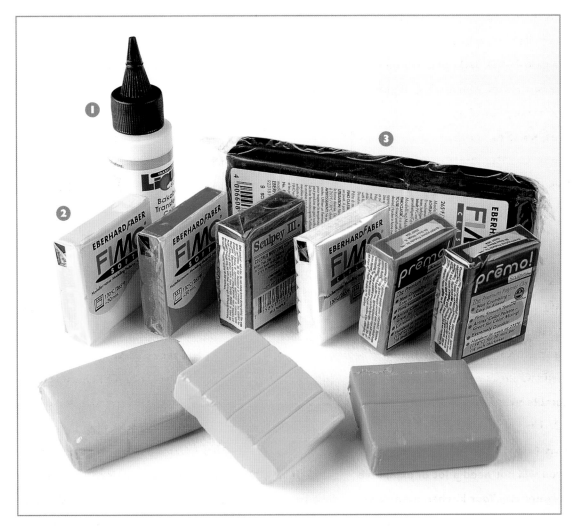

Polymer clay is produced by many different manufacturers in a variety of colors and formulations.
1 *Liquid polymer clay.*
2 *Standard polymer clay blocks weigh around 60 g (2 oz).*
3 *Larger blocks are also available from some manufacturers.*

Color range, smoothability and the tensile strength when baked are factors to consider when making your selection. Also consider how soft the clay is in use and how easy it is to knead or condition to that soft, workable state fresh from the packet (see page 13). Most manufacturers package polymer clay in standard sized blocks, weighing approximately 60 g (2 oz). Here are a few guidelines to the best known brands and types of clay product available.

Fimo Classic (Eberhard Faber, Germany) is often considered difficult to condition although the formulation has changed recently making it much easier to prepare. It stays firm as you work with it, holding detail well, and is semi-smoothable. Fimo Classic comes in a basic color palette designed to be blended into custom colors. It is strong when baked. **Fimo Soft** is very easy to condition and comes in a larger range than the Classic formulation, with many speciality colors. It is more smoothable than Fimo Classic but slightly less strong when baked.

Fimo Mix Quick is a solid kneading medium that can help soften the clay and also make it more flexible when baked.

Premo! Sculpey (Polyform Products, USA) is soft, smoothable and quick to condition. Colors are based on a traditional artist's palette for easy color mixing and include a much loved range of metallics. When baked it is strong and thin sheets become very flexible. **Sculpey III** is very soft, smoothable and conditions easily. When baked it is brittle and therefore not suitable for very fine or thin items. However it is superb for more solid projects and has a wide palette including pearlized colors. **Sculpey Clay Softener** is a liquid softener that can be used to soften firm clay, make clay grouts and aid in surface smoothing.

Cernit (T& F Kunststoffe, Germany) is a firm clay that conditions quickly to become very soft in use, but is not smoothable. It is semi-translucent, which gives a porcelain-like effect when baked, popular with sculptors and doll makers. Colors include a wide range of flesh tones as well as metallic and pearlized clays. It is one of the strongest clays when baked.

Other polymer clay brands you might find are Creall-Therm, Du-Kit, Friendly Clay, Kato PolyClay, Modello / Formello, Modelene, Uro.

LIQUID POLYMER CLAY

Liquid polymer clay has multiple uses. Best known are the translucent versions such as Translucent Liquid Sculpey (Polyform). These mediums have the consistency of honey, remaining fluid until baked. Although not totally transparent, applying in thin layers will allow you to see through to the surface beneath. Liquid clays can be colored with metallic powders or oil paints and used decoratively. They can also be used to create transfers, repair cracks and when baked will form a strong adhesive bond between separate pieces of clay.

SCRAP CLAY

Scrap clay is a term used to describe the odds and ends of clay left over from your projects. Keep every bit of this scrap clay; although it becomes an unattractive color when mixed together, it is still valuable. You can decorate scrap clay with foils and paints or use it in projects where the clay will not be visible, such as inside beads. It is so handy in fact, you will even find artists and companies that buy and sell scrap clay! There are several projects in this book that call for scrap so you will not be short of ideas on how to put it to use.

STORING POLYMER CLAY

Although it becomes firmer over time, when stored correctly your clay will stay usable for years. Keep un-baked clay cool and out of bright sunlight. Opened packets can be kept in polythene reclosable sandwich bags or wrapped in baking parchment to keep the clay clean and dust free. Beware of leaving un-baked clay on plastic surfaces. The plasticizers in the clay can soften some plastics and the two will end up melded together. The plasticizers will also leach out on to normal paper, so do not wrap clay in paper bags or cardboard. However, leaching the plasticizer in this way can be done purposely if you wish to stiffen up clay that is too soft. To do this, place sheets of clay in between layers of plain paper, weighing it down with a book, and leave overnight.

BAKING OR CURING

Your creations are permanently hardened by baking in a domestic oven, usually at 130°C/275°F for around half an hour. Baking requirements can vary from brand to brand however, so always follow the instructions on the clay packaging. Place items directly on to a ceramic tile or use a baking sheet lined with baking parchment. Place in a pre-heated oven or a dedicated toaster oven and always use an independent oven thermometer to verify the temperature; the in-built thermostats in ovens are often inaccurate. It is important that your work bakes for the correct amount of time at the correct temperature. If you under-bake your work it will be weak, if you exceed the recommended temperature you risk burning the clay which can release toxic fumes, not to mention ruining all your hard work! Do not let this scare you; I have only accidentally burned clay once in many years of using it! Just treat the baking process with respect and take care to bake the clay accurately.

The clay can be baked many times over. Multiple baking in this way can be very useful, allowing you to add legs to sculptures or build a complex vessel in stages. If adding un-baked clay to baked clay, smearing a little liquid polymer clay between the two pieces will form a strong bond during the subsequent second baking. Finally, be aware that baked clay only becomes hard once it has cooled so allow items to cool completely before handling.

SANDING, BUFFING AND VARNISHING

Sanding the baked clay is not necessary but doing so will remove unsightly fingerprints and rough edges and give a more finished look to your work. Use wet/dry sandpaper and sand underwater to prevent creating clouds of fine polymer clay dust, starting with coarser grit papers and progressing through to finer grits until you achieved a smooth finish. A 400 or 600 grit paper is a good starting point if the surface is already quite even, but you may wish to begin with coarser paper if the surface needs a lot of refining. Items can then be left with their natural finish, buffed to a high sheen or varnished. Most polymer clay manufacturers produce their own range of varnishes but you can also use some other brands of acrylic varnish. Do not use solvent-based or any aerosol varnishes as often they do not dry properly or may react with the clay over time.

Projects using foils or powders as a surface decoration cannot be sanded or buffed. Instead, you should varnish them to protect the decorated surface from flaking or tarnishing.

Wet-sand baked clay in a small basin of water. A drop of detergent added to the water can help keep the sandpaper clog-free.

Varnishing baked clay can bring out the colors and protect surface decorations. Use a soft brush and apply the varnish in smooth, even coats.

Safety advice

Polymer clay is certified as non-toxic when used in accordance with the manufacturers' instructions. Always keep and refer to the safety recommendations printed on the packaging. Some manufacturers produce separate leaflets with more comprehensive safety advice which you can ask your retailer for. Remember:

❋ Polymer clay can burn and release toxic fumes if baked above the recommended temperature. If you accidentally burn your clay, (indicated by a terrible smell!) turn off the oven and removed the burned clay. Ventilate the room well and keep out until the fumes have cleared. Never let children or pets stay unsupervised in a room where clay is being baked.

❋ Do not allow baked or un-baked clay to come in contact with food. Baked clay should not be considered food-safe, so do not use it to make serving bowls. When using your kitchen oven for baking clay, it is recommended that you clean it well after use. Never bake clay and food in the oven at the same time!

❋ Always wash your hands well after working with polymer clay. Never put clay in your mouth.

❋ Never put clay into a microwave oven. It may seem like a good idea at the time, but it isn't. Microwaves do not heat evenly and can quickly heat areas of the clay beyond the recommended temperatures, causing it to burn and release dangerous fumes.

Tools and Additional Materials

You need very few tools to work with polymer clay. At first you will need little more than a smooth, non-porous work surface and simple tools to roll, cut and pierce the clay. As you progress you may wish to invest in more exciting gadgets! These are the tools that I find most useful, although you are bound to discover your own favorites. Mail order companies can supply any tool that you can't buy locally (see page 79).

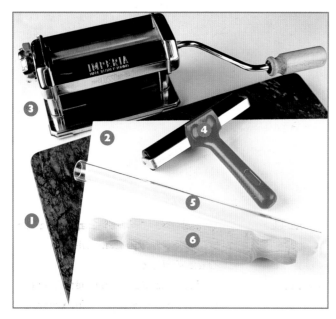

Work surfaces and rolling tools **1** *marble slab* **2** *large ceramic tile* **3** *pasta machine* **4** *brayer* **5** *acrylic rod* **6** *rolling pin*

Cutting tools **1** *tissue blades* **2** *craft knives* **3** *cookie and canapé cutters*

WORK SURFACES

❀ **Marble slab** Marble makes a good work surface as it is smooth and is naturally quite cold. This is useful if you need the clay to stay cool and firm.

❀ **Ceramic tile** Ceramic tiles make wonderful work surfaces. They can be placed into the oven, so you can work directly on the tile and then bake the project without having to disturb it.

ROLLING TOOLS

❀ **Hand rollers** A smooth rolling pin, acrylic rod or brayer can all be used to roll clay by hand.

❀ **Pasta machine** This wonderful machine rolls sheets at various thicknesses. Use it also for conditioning and color mixing. It is not essential, but is a real investment if you plan to do a lot of polymer clay work.

CUTTING TOOLS

❀ **Tissue blades** These long, thin and flexible blades are perfect for cutting straight and curved lines in sheets of clay or cutting slices from canes.

❀ **Craft knife** Use for more detailed cutting.

❀ **Cookie and canapé cutters** Great for cutting interesting shapes.

SHAPING AND FORMING TOOLS

❀ **Clay gun** This clever device comes with multiple dies to extrude lengths of clay in different shapes. Unfortunately it can be difficult to use with firm clays. Adding clay softeners to the clay will help, as can holding the gun plunger-side down against the floor and pushing down on the handles with your feet!

❀ **Piercing tools** Use needle tools, wooden toothpicks and skewers to pierce clay before baking. A mini hand drill can be used to drill through baked clay.

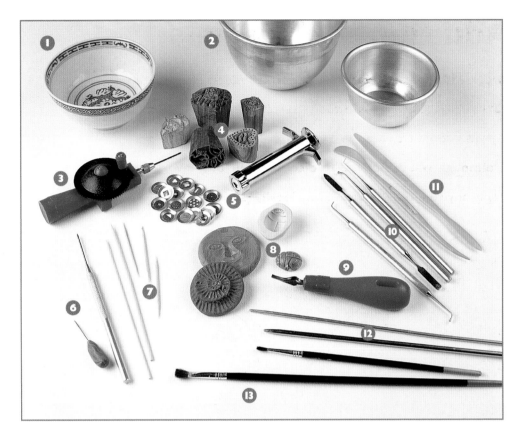

Shaping and forming tools

1 *china bowl*

2 *metal bowls*

3 *mini hand drill*

4 *wooden printing blocks*

5 *clay gun and dies*

6 *needle tools*

7 *wooden skewers and toothpicks*

8 *home-made molds*

9 *linoleum cutter*

10 *dental tools*

11 *modelling tools*

12 *knitting needles*

13 *paintbrushes*

❧ **Modelling and dental tools** Use for adding detail to sculpture or other delicate work. Different sized knitting needles are also very useful.

❧ **Bowls and plates** Use metal or china bowls and plates as forms for clay vessels, removing when the clay has baked and cooled.

❧ **Texture tools** Rubber stamps, wooden printing blocks, buttons, texture sheets and fabric are superb for adding texture to un-baked clay.

❧ **Linoleum cutter** Can be used to carve baked clay.

❧ **Molds** Buy ready made molds or make your own (see page 22).

OTHER USEFUL TOOLS

❧ **Paintbrushes and soft cosmetic brushes**

❧ **Pliers**

❧ **Baking sheet** Line with baking parchment and use for baking clay projects in the oven.

❧ **Metal ruler and calipers** Use a metal ruler for measuring against clay, plastic ones tend to react with the clay. Calipers are also useful to measure clay sheets and balls.

DECORATING MATERIALS

There are many other supplies useful both in the decoration and indeed the very construction of polymer clay projects. Keep your eyes open in art and craft shops, hardware stores and even thrift, second hand shops and garage sales. You never know when you will find something useful that can be used in your projects. It is worthwhile building up a little hoard of treasures like these!

❧ **Metal Leaf and Foils** Decorative and precious metal leaf look wonderful applied to polymer clay. Lay a sheet of un-baked clay directly on to the metal leaf and lift up. Gently smooth the leaf on the clay with a soft brush. Rolling this sheet will give a crackled effect.

Some plastic backed metallic foils can also be used. Lay the foil colored side up on the clay and burnish well by scraping with the edge of a tissue blade. Rip the plastic backing away from the clay leaving the foil in place.

❧ **Powders** Beautiful surface decorations can be achieved by stamping or brushing un-baked clay with colored bronze and mica powders. These are decorative artists' powders for general arts and crafts use, available in a variety of metallic colors. Unusual effects can also be created by mixing the powders into the clay (this can be especially effective if using translucent clay). Colored sand, embossing powders, powdered artist's pastels and glitter are also fun to use as an inclusion or surface decoration.

✤ **Paint Products** Acrylic paints can be applied to either baked or un-baked clay. You can also find acrylic paint and patina ranges containing real metals that will transform baked clay to mimic rusty iron or copper with a verdigris patina. Acrylic artists' inks can also be used on un-baked clay to create wonderful effects, especially those in metallic colors. Do not use solvent-based or enamel paints however as they are not compatible with polymer clay. Many oil paints are also problematic with standard polymer clays, so save these for coloring liquid clay only.

✤ **Embellishments** Small polished stones, glass nuggets, beads, buttons, shells and rhinestones are just a few of the objects you can embed into the clay surface (see page 22). Make sure anything you choose can withstand the baking temperature. Look out at second hand shops for old beads and junk jewelery to dismantle. Magpies have nothing on polymer clay artists for collecting shiny things!

ARMATURES AND "COVERABLE" OBJECTS

Wire mesh and aluminum foil can be formed into armatures then covered in clay, perfect for larger items where weight is a factor or you wish to save on clay. Thin metal sheet and embossing foils can also be cut to shape and covered. PVC pipe, which is available from DIY stores or hardware stores, cardboard and wooden boxes, drinking glasses, bottles, metal tins and blown eggshells can all tolerate the baking temperature and therefore be covered in clay and transformed into beautiful, original objects.

Decorating materials 1 *plastic-backed foils* **2** *decorative metal leaf* **3** *metal sheet and embossing foils* **4** *wire mesh* **5** *acrylic paints* **6** *colored bronze and mica powders* **7** *embossing powders* **8** *small polished stones* **9** *glass rhinestones, small pearls and shells* **10** *glass nuggets* **11** *colored craft wires*

GLUES AND OTHER SUNDRIES

Use white PVA glue when attaching baked clay to wood, paper or card and as a primer to attach un-baked clay to other surfaces. Cyanoacrylate glues (superglue) and epoxy glues are best for sticking baked clay to glass and metal and can be used to glue baked clay pieces together.

Keep some methylated spirit or rubbing alcohol for degreasing work surfaces, cleaning tools and also to clean baked and un-baked clay. Talcum powder or cornstarch is useful as a release for molds or for dusting on to blades and cutters to lessen drag. Also keep a roll of baking parchment to hand for lining baking sheets and wrapping clay, and a roll of plastic sandwich wrap for creating bevelled effects when cutting clay.

Getting Started

Whatever you choose to make, you will nearly always need to form the basic shapes – sheets, logs and balls, at some point. Many polymer clay projects are indeed no more technical than just this, and are simply about making and combining these shapes in a variety of ways. However, although the core shapes are simple, the results you can achieve with them are anything but!

CONDITIONING

All polymer clays needs to be kneaded or conditioned a little prior to use. Conditioning makes the clay soft and pliable; it also ensures the different ingredients in the clay are well mixed together. Cut thin slices from the block of clay and run several times through a pasta machine until the clay is soft enough to combine without crumbling. To condition by hand, roll the clay into a log shape, fold it in half and continue rolling. Repeat this until the clay no longer cracks or crumbles when you fold it. Fresh clay will usually condition quickly. To condition older, firmer clay try adding some clay softener following the directions for use on the packaging.

Do not over condition the clay. As soon as the clay is soft enough to shape and folds easily without crumbling it is ready for use and you can proceed with your project.

ROLLING SHEETS

Using a pasta machine is the easiest way to roll uniform sheets of clay. Select the thickest setting using the dial on the side of the machine. Form the conditioned clay into a flat piece that is not too thick and feed it into the rollers as you crank the handle. You can then roll the sheet thinner

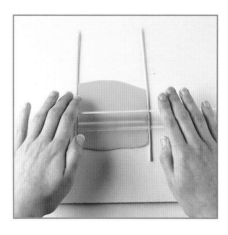

Rest the roller on top of guide rods when hand rolling to create a sheet of even thickness.

by selecting a different setting and re-rolling the sheet. Pasta machines do vary, so make test tiles using your machine to see what thickness each setting will give.

Sheets can also be rolled by hand using a suitable hand roller. Rolling along guide rods set either side of the clay will ensure the sheet is an even thickness all over. Wooden skewers made good guides for thicker sheets and strips of card or wood can be used for thinner sheets.

ROLLING LOGS

Form the clay into a rough log shape with your hands and then roll it back and forth on the work surface to make it even. Use the entire length of your fingers, moving you hands apart and back again along the log as you roll. By doing this no part of the log gets too much pressure. This will, with

practice, result in a smooth, even log. For thin strings of clay continue the process until the desired diameter is achieved, using your fingertips to roll the string as it gets thinner. Certain diameter logs and strings can also be extruded from the clay gun.

Move your hands from side to side as well as back and forth to roll evenly shaped logs.

Form round balls by rolling the clay between your palms.

Pierce from each side into the middle to make a neat hole.

MAKING BALLS

Clay balls are fundamental to many projects. Often you will want to make several of the same size, for example when you are making beads. Roll a log of clay and cut it into equal sections (measure with a metal ruler against the log as you cut.) Take each section in turn and form it into a rough sphere with your fingers then roll it between your palms in a circular motion to perfect the shape. As with rolling logs, it will take practice to find the exact amount of pressure needed to roll near-perfect round balls.

PIERCING BALLS

Correct piercing is also important if you are using the clay balls to make beads. Use a needle tool, wooden toothpick or skewer and twist it gently halfway into the ball. Remove the piercing tool and repeat from the other side, twisting into the clay until the holes meet in the middle. If this does not sound like your idea of fun, you can drill the beads after baking to make the threading holes instead.

COLOR MIXING

Although polymer clay comes in many different "off the shelf" colors, you can also mix these together to form countless more. Colors are mixed in the same way that the clay is conditioned, so by mixing your own colors you are preparing the clay as you go! Roll the clays you wish to mix into logs and twist them together. Fold the twisted clay in half, and roll it back into a log. Either repeat the process until the colors are completely blended or stop for beautifully marbled clay. Keep notes of the proportions you use of each color when mixing. Then you will be able to easily make the new color again.

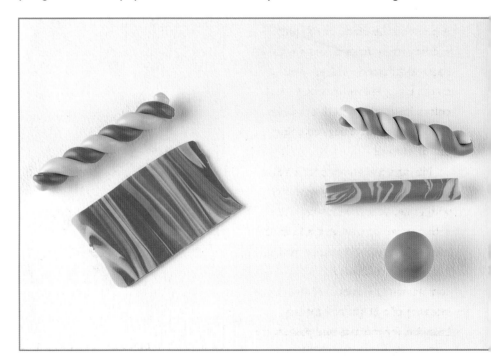

When mixing colors together, the clays become marbleized, then completely blended.

The traditional primary colors and the secondary colors that can be mixed from them.

As with paints, you can actually mix any possible color using only the three primary colors. Traditionally the primary colors are red, yellow and blue. Mix red and yellow to make orange, yellow and blue to make green and mix blue and red to make violet. Use a little white and black clay to lighten and darken the colors.

Some clay artists prefer instead to mix their colors from the primaries used in printing; magenta, cyan and yellow. Getting good secondary colors from these printer's primaries will depend on the brand of clay you use and how true those colors are to begin with. Brands with very pure colors can give lovely secondary colors from the printer's primaries although a good strong red color can be elusive!

Mixing equal amounts of a color with its complementary color (red with green, yellow with violet, blue with orange) usually results in earthy browns and grays. However, mixing in just a small touch of the complementary color can reduce the intensity of a bright color nicely. Likewise, for more muted pastels, try adding colors to a base of flesh-colored clay instead of white.

COLORING TRANSLUCENT CLAYS

Some of the projects in this book require pre-colored translucent clay, such as the Wine Glass Charmers on page 29. This is easily done by mixing in a little colored clay to the translucent while you are conditioning it. You need only a very small amount of colored clay to tinge the translucent, adding too much can lessen its translucent properties. Bear in mind also that colored translucent clays often become darker when baked. So play around with proportions, making and baking a few test tiles to get a feel of how these clays behave.

CHOOSING COLORS

You should experiment not only to find new colors, but also exciting color combinations. The colors you choose can have dramatic effects on your work and the emotions it creates in anyone who views it. Soft pastels or cool icy colors might relax for example, while warm and fiery combinations are more likely to stimulate and excite.

Projects using colors that are similar, such as greens and blues, can be perked up by adding accents of their complementary colors. The two clay pins below show the difference that using a complementary color accent (in this case red) can make.

Think also about the "value" of the colors you use, or how light and dark they are compared to each other. Colors of a similar value will not be so vibrant when used together as those with contrasting values. Try to imagine colors as they would appear in a black and white photograph – would all your colors be similar shades of gray or would there be a good mix of light and dark? Contrast is especially important in smaller items where detail can be easily lost, such as millefiore cane patterns (see pages 16-18).

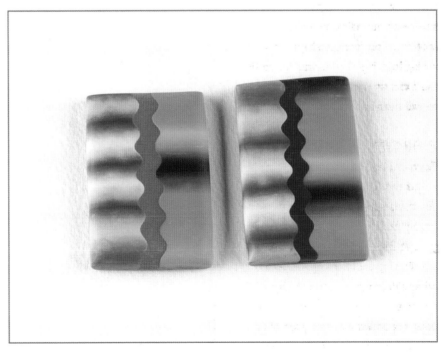

Complementary colors used as accents add excitement to the design.

Millefiore Cane Techniques

Millefiore canes are long logs of clay that reveal intricate patterns or pictures in the cross section when cut. Slices from these canes can be used to make patterned sheets of clay and beads, or used to decorate objects. Millefiore (literally "thousand flowers") is an Italian term describing glassware made using an age-old process that was the inspiration behind this popular polymer clay technique.

Bull's eye cane: Sheets of different colored clay are wrapped around a central log.

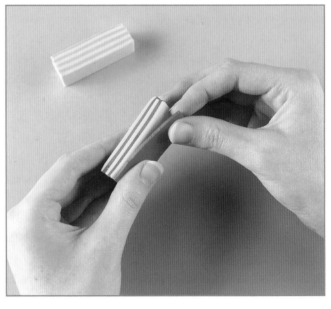

Striped cane: Strips of two contrasting colors are stacked on top of each other.

Millefiore canes are easily made from polymer clay by combining clay sheets, logs and other shapes, fitted together to build the picture or pattern that we wish to see when the cane is cut. These canes can be reduced, lengthening the cane and making the pattern smaller. They can also be combined to make more complex or repeating patterns.

Use the same brand of clay throughout when making canes, firm clays often give better results than soft clays which can distort very easily. Avoid using stone effect clay which contains small fibers or clay with large glitter particles as canes made from these clays will smear when you try to cut them. When making canes for the first time it is a good idea to use shades of the same color, such as light, medium and dark blue. Then if you do not like the results you can mix the clays together again and still have a usable color. Below are a few simple and combined canes, you will find other examples of canework in the projects throughout the book.

SIMPLE CANES

❋ **Bull's Eye cane** Form a clay log and a sheet from a contrasting color. Trim a neat edge to the sheet and wrap it around the log. Where the sheet overlaps, trim away the excess and butt the two cut edges together neatly. Continue to wrap the cane in further layers if you wish.

❋ **Striped cane** Cut matching strips from two different colored clay sheets. Stack the strips on top of each other, alternating the colors, to form a striped cane. You can also cut this cane in half lengthways and stack the sections on top of each other to create a narrower cane with more layers. To keep the lines precise, it is best not to reduce these canes.

Spiral or Jellyroll cane: Strips of different colored clay are rolled up together forming a spiral.

Cookie cutter canes: Sections cut from the middle of two clay patties are switched around, making two co-ordinating canes.

Checkerboard cane: Logs are used to form the pattern, becoming square-shaped when pushed together.

✣ **Spiral or Jellyroll cane** Stack two different colored strips of clay on top of each other. Taper one end of the stack by flattening it with your fingertips. Starting from this end, roll the clay up into a spiral or jellyroll shape. Before you finish rolling, cut the final end of the stack at an angle, this allows the outer colored sheet to wrap around the cane neatly.

✣ **Cookie cutter cane** Form circular patties from two different colored clays – contrasting colors work best. Cut a shape from the middle of each using a cookie or canapé cutter and then switch the cut out sections around. Push the clay together and voilà! Two coordinating canes in an instant which can be reduced further if you wish.

✣ **Checkerboard cane** Roll logs from two different colored clays and combine as shown. The logs will naturally become square shaped when the cane is pinched together and reduced. Use different colored logs together to form mosaic canes or combine triangle- and square-shaped logs to make quilt patterns.

REDUCING CANES

Everyone develops their own particular method for reducing canes, but most artists include pinching, squeezing, stretching and even wringing the cane in their arsenal of techniques. But the aim is always the same; to make the cane longer and thinner, so that the pattern in the cross section becomes smaller.

Canes will reduce better if all the clays within them are of the same consistency and preferably cool and firm. Chilling canes in the refrigerator before reducing is a good way to ensure this. When reducing large or awkward size canes, take breaks periodically to let the clay cool down.

So, the way to reduce your canes is to pinch them and stretch them until they become longer and thinner. Round canes can also be rolled carefully along the work surface to neaten. For triangle- or square-shaped canes you can neaten each side in turn with a hand roller. After reduction, the ends of a cane will always be a little distorted so trim these away and save them for your scrap clay pile.

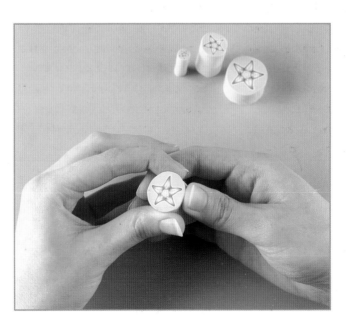

Reducing canes: Pinch the cane along its length, making it longer and thinner.

COMPLEX CANES AND PICTURE CANES

Canes can be combined to make more complex patterns as well. Picture canes can also be made by forming the different components and assembling them together like a jigsaw puzzle. When designing your own complex canes bear in mind that as the cane is reduced the clays inside will fill up any gaps or spaces, as in the checkerboard cane. If there is an element within your cane that you wish to maintain a certain shape, it is important that you pack around that element well. The two variations of a flower cane below illustrate this.

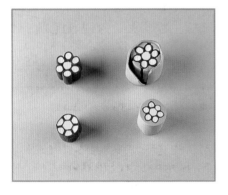

Flower canes: Retain the round shape of the petals by packing the gaps with a different color clay.

❀ **Flower canes** In the first cane, six sections of a bull's eye cane have been arranged around a yellow log to form a simple flower. When reduced, the outer canes splay out and loose their round shape. In the second version, small triangle sections of clay have been placed in between the outer canes filling the gaps. The cane has then been wrapped with a strip of matching clay. When this cane is reduced, the "petals" retain their shape and the clay that was used to fill the gaps becomes the background.

Picture canes: Combining sections of clay like a jigsaw puzzle is an easy way to make picture canes.

❀ **Picture cane** Irregular patterns and pictures like this tree cane can be built, combining clay pieces like a jigsaw puzzle. I designed the cane on paper and then cut templates out for the main features. Colored slabs of clay were made by stacking several sheets on top of each other. The sections were then cut from the slabs and combined together. The cane was allowed to rest, and then reduced.

TRANSLUCENT CLAYS IN CANES

Canes can also be made using translucent clays. Taking very thin slices from these canes and overlapping them will allow you to see through to the layer below. The effect becomes apparent when the clay is sanded and then buffed or varnished. I first saw this lovely technique in an article by clay artist Donna Kato where she used it to make stunning beads that looked like glass. It has also been used by many other artists to create spectacular results and is put to good use in the Multi-Layered Pens project (see page 66). You will find the technique most effective if the canes contain both translucent and opaque clay elements.

Slicing canes: Use a sharp blade to cut canes, keeping the blade upright as you push down.

SLICING CANES

Cool canes in the refrigerator before slicing as firm clay will cut more easily. Use a sharp tissue blade, holding it upright as you cut down, and rotate the cane after each cut to prevent it becoming flat along the bottom. Take great care when using sharp blades or craft knives; accidents can easily happen if your fingers stray too close to the blade.

Thick slices can be pierced to make beads and pendants. Apply thinner cane slices to logs of scrap clay and roll smooth. Sections can then be cut and pierced to make patterned tube beads. Cover balls of scrap clay in the same way and pierce to make round beads (see page 14).

Cover small sections of scrap clay with cane slices and roll smooth to create different types of beads.

The Skinner Blend Technique

A Skinner blend is a sheet of clay forming a perfect gradation of two or more colors. These blends, named after artist Judith Skinner who devised the technique, have infinite uses. You can roll a Skinner blend by hand using a hand roller and guides, but it is certainly labor-saving to use a pasta machine. Several projects in this book benefit from this ingenious process – practice making some Skinner blends and you will soon be hooked by all the different possible color combinations!

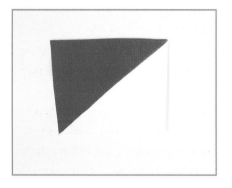

1 Form triangles from different colored sheets and position into a rectangle.

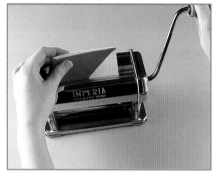

2 Fold the rectangle top to bottom and run, fold first, through the pasta machine.

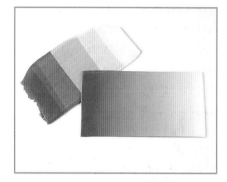

3 Fold and roll several times; the sheet will become striped then blended.

BASIC PROCEDURE

1 Cut right-angled triangles from two different colored sheets of clay and position into a rectangle as shown.
2 Fold this rectangle in half along the horizontal axis. Place, fold first, into the pasta machine and roll on the thickest setting. Continue folding and rolling the sheet, always folding in the same direction.
3 After several repetitions the sheet will start to become striped and then completely blended.

If you are rolling by hand, always place the folded edge nearest to you and roll forwards and backwards, do not turn the sheet or roll from side to side.

SKINNER BLEND ROLLS AND LOAVES

You may want to lengthen the blend, forming a long strip rather that a sheet. This is especially useful if you want to incorporate Skinner blends into canes. Fold the blended sheet along the horizontal axis as you would normally. This time pass through the

pasta machine or hand roll from the narrow end of the folded sheet, making the blend thinner and longer. This strip can then be rolled up to make a gradated bull's eye cane or used in jellyroll canes. Alternatively you can make a loaf of Skinner blended clay by folding up the strip in an accordian fashion.

Skinner Blends can add unique shading and depth to canes. Lengthening the blend is useful when using Skinner blends in this way.

Mokume Gane Techniques

Mokume Gane (literally "wood grain metal") is a Japanese metalworking technique adapted for use with polymer clay. Thin layers of different colored clays are formed into a slab. The clay slab is then manipulated by various methods so that slices taken from the top reveal unique patterns. You can then use the patterned slab in different projects and the slices can be used decoratively too.

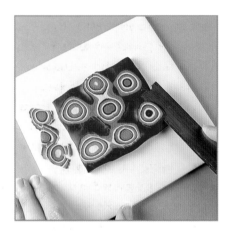

Slice away the raised areas of the Mokume Gane slab to reveal the patterns.

Different effects can be achieved by indenting the slab with cutters and stamps.

Roll several thin sheets of different colored clays and stack them to form a striped slab roughly 1 cm (⅜ in) tall. Slabs can also be made using very thin layers of translucent clays with decorative metal leaf sandwiched between. Translucent Mokume Gane slabs give breathtaking effects, very different from using only opaque clays. A translucent variation is shown in the Fluorite Mokume Egg project on page 48. Whatever type of slab you make for your Mokume Gane, the layers must then be altered by one of the following methods to create the patterns.

"HILLS AND VALLEYS" METHOD

This method will give the traditional circular patterned Mokume Gane. Roll several clay balls about 15 mm (⅝ in) diameter from the same colors used in the slab. (You can marble together clay left from forming the slab to do this.) Position the balls randomly on the slab, leaving space around each one. Turn the slab over and push down the clay all around the balls, creating high and low areas in the slab. You can achieve the same result by simply indenting the underside of the slab with a rounded tool, although with this method it can be a little more difficult to cut slices as there is nothing below the raised areas to offer support.

INDENTING METHOD

Different patterns can be created by indenting the slab from above rather than below. You can get interesting effects by pressing canapé cutters into the surface. Try laying a sheet of plastic sandwich wrap over the slab first so the cutters indent rather than cut the clay. Indenting the slab with different tools such as a ball stylus or the end of a pencil also produces interesting patterns.

Rubber stamps pushed into the surface of the slab will make spectacular effects. Small wooden printing blocks work even better as they are often deeper cut than rubber stamps and make a stronger image.

To reveal the patterns, use a sharp tissue blade held horizontally and take thin slices from across the top of the slab. Cut all the slices you will need and set them aside on some parchment paper. Every slice from a Mokume Gane slab is unique and quite often the first few slices will be the most dramatic. You may wish to save these initial slices to use last on a project, so they become the focal point rather than the background.

Additional Techniques

There are many other polymer clay techniques for you to use aside from those we have already looked at. Here is a quick guide to creating some effects that you may wish to incorporate into your work. You will find more ideas in the projects that follow too!

IMITATING NATURAL MATERIALS

Polymer clay can be used to imitate many different natural materials. For a realistic looking turquoise, chill some conditioned turquoise-colored clay until it is firm. Chop the clay roughly into small chunks and then carefully press into shape without smoothing away the texture. Bake the clay as normal and allow it to cool, then coat with brown acrylic paint. When the paint has dried, wet-sand the clay to reveal a realistic looking turquoise complete with brown matrix.

Faux jade can be made by using green-colored translucent clay. Grate small crumbs of dark brown clay and push these into the surface to mimic the natural impurities often seen in real jade. Agate and marble can be easily simulated by marbling together different colored opaque and translucent clays.

To emulate ivory and bone, bundle logs of translucent and ivory colored clay together. Roll and fold the log several times then slice lengthways to reveal the "grain". Place sections of the sliced log side by side and roll into a sheet. By varying the colors, you can also mimic wood with this method.

HIGHLIGHTING TEXTURES

When adding texture to your work you can do several things to make the effect more pronounced. One way is to apply a little mica or colored bronze powders to the raised areas with your fingertip. The clay can also be "antiqued" by painting the baked piece with dark brown acrylic paint. Either wipe the wet paint from the raised areas or sand back once the paint is dry. This works beautifully on light colored clay such as faux bone and ivory pieces.

GLAZING

An imitation glaze is another way to highlight textures on baked polymer clay. This works very well with molded items as the "glaze" will settle in hollows and appear darker. Use white polymer clay to create the object. When baked, paint the clay with coats of watered down acrylic paints until you reach the desired color. When the paint is dry, varnish the clay or alternatively paint it with a damp paintbrush and sprinkle with clear embossing powder. Return the item to the oven until the powder has melted, then remove and allow to cool. The blue paperweight was made from white polymer clay and glazed using this method.

Translucent liquid polymer clay can be colored with oil paints to create a matt glazed look. Paint it over the baked clay and then re-bake the piece to cure the liquid clay glaze.

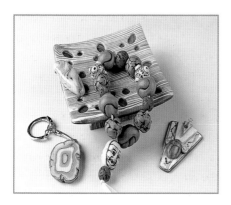

It is possible to imitate many natural materials using polymer clay.

Textures can be enhanced by highlighting with powders or antiquing with paints.

Acrylic paints and embossing powders can be used to emulate colored glazes.

Using molds is an easy way to create beads, buttons and decorative details for a number of projects.

MAKING AND USING MOLDS

There are many push-molds produced specifically for polymer clay use but you can also make your own. Use scrap clay to make molds from buttons, beads or other small objects. You can then use these molds to replicate the object over and over. Dust the object that you wish to reproduce with talcum powder and push it into a flattened ball of scrap clay. Remove the object carefully and bake the mold. To use the mold, first dust the inside with talcum powder to act as a release. Form a ball of clay and roll it into a cone shape. Push the thin end of the cone into the deepest part of the mold and carry on pushing until the mold is full. You can then slice the excess clay away and remove the impression from the mold by tapping it firmly on a table top. To make flexible molds, experiment with RTV (Room Temperature Vulcanizing) molding compounds, available from jewelery-making supplies stores. Many RTV compounds can tolerate heat, allowing you to bake the clay in the mold and remove it afterwards.

EMBEDDING OBJECTS

Many different objects can be embedded into the clay surface providing they can withstand the heat of baking. Small embellishments such as beads and glass rhinestones can be pushed directly into the clay, although you may need to glue them back into place after baking if they seem loose. For larger items such as polished stones or cabochons place a little PVA glue or liquid polymer clay on to the back and position on the clay. You can

Many different items can be incorporated into projects as a surface embellishment.

then edge the stone with a small string of clay to form a bevel and dust with metallic powders if you like. If you use glass nuggets as an embellishment, back the glass with a thin sheet of white or foiled clay. This will make the color of the glass more noticeable in the finished piece.

TRANSFERRING IMAGES

Black and white images printed on to paper with toner (from a photocopier or laser printer) can be transferred to polymer clay. Place a sheet of white or light colored clay on to a ceramic tile and cut to size. Lay the image face down on to the clay and burnish well to ensure all the image is touching the clay surface. Place in the oven and bake as normal. When the clay has cooled enough to handle, remove the paper. The image will be permanently transferred and you can then incorporate the clay piece into other projects. If you coat the clay first with a thin layer of liquid polymer clay and

Liquid polymer clay can be used to increase the saturation of transferred images.

then lay the transfer, you will get a more saturated image.

For colored images, color the black and white transfers with coloring pencils and the color will transfer in the same way that the toner does. If you have an inkjet color printer, you can also print color images on to certain brands of T-shirt transfer paper and transfer on to polymer clay using the same methods. Note that when you transfer images they will appear reversed.

Liquid polymer clay can been used to create decoupage effects.

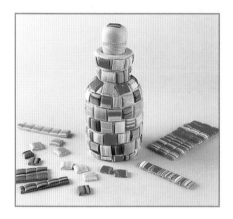

Mosaic tiles in any shape or color are made easily from polymer clay.

MOSAICS

Polymer clay is superb for making mosaic tiles and tesserae. There are many different methods for doing this but here is my favorite. Roll some marbled clay into a sheet 3 mm (⅛ in) thick and place on to a ceramic tile. Lay a sheet of plastic sandwich wrap over the clay and using a tissue blade, push down firmly through the clay, forming a grid pattern to make the tiles. The plastic wrap will give the individual tiles a bevelled edge. (If you do not want bevelled tiles just cut straight into the clay.) Bake the clay on the ceramic tile and when cool you will be able to snap apart the individual tiles. You can push the tiles

directly into a base of un-baked clay, coated with liquid polymer clay to aid adhesion, then bake again to cure the base layer. The bottle pictured was made this way. Tiles can also be glued directly on to surfaces, using PVA or epoxy glue. You can make tiles in any shape or size using this method. Try using canapé cutters for interesting features or cut random, freehand lines for a "crazy quilt" style mosaic.

You can even make polymer clay grouts for your mosaics by diluting some clay with liquid clay softener to form a thick paste. Apply the paste over the mosaic, pushing it into the gaps between the tiles then lightly sponge clean the surface with a couple of drops of the liquid softener. Liquid polymer clay can also be used as a grout. Apply the liquid clay into the gaps between the tiles and then

carefully wipe the surface clean. Whichever method you use, do not forget to bake the item afterwards to cure the grout!

DÉCOUPAGE

Decorative papers, pieces of fine fabrics and even pressed flowers can all be used to decorate clay using découpage techniques. The bookmarks pictured above were made by placing dried, pressed flowers on to thin clay sheets. The clay and flowers were covered with a thin layer of translucent liquid polymer clay, and then baked and varnished.

If you are using paper or fabric, apply a coat of translucent liquid polymer clay to both the back and the front before applying it to the clay surface, baking afterwards. A coat of varnish will bring out the colors.

Surprise Greeting Cards

These floral greeting cards are easy to make and are much more personal than giving a shop-bought card. They also contain a surprise gift! The decoration on the card is a fridge magnet that can be removed once the celebrations are over and kept as a lasting memento. The project makes use of the Skinner blend and simple millefiore cane techniques to create these elegant flowers. You can adapt the technique to create cards for Christmas, Valentine's Day or any other holiday.

Skill level
✳ ✳ ✳

You will need

❀ ½ block red polymer clay

❀ ½ block white polymer clay

❀ ¼ block scrap polymer clay

❀ ⅛ block yellow polymer clay

❀ Pasta machine or hand roller

❀ 15 x 10 cm (6 x 4 in) greeting card blank with aperture

❀ Tissue blade

❀ Small round canapé cutter

❀ Small ceramic tile

❀ Wooden skewer or ball stylus

❀ Epoxy two-part glue

❀ Magnet

❀ Double-sided adhesive tape

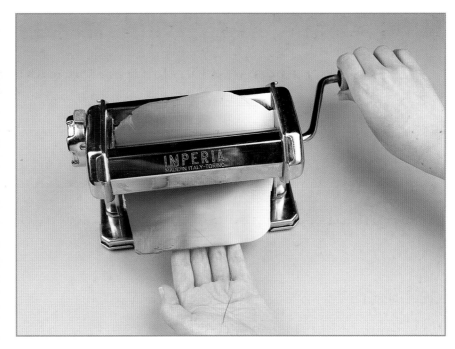

1 Roll the red and the white clay into sheets each 3 mm (⅛ in) thick. From the sheets form two right-angled triangles. Create a Skinner blend sheet from the triangles approximately 3 mm (⅛ in) thick, following the directions shown on page 19.

2 Lengthen the blend by folding the sheet in half and, starting with the narrow edge first, either feed into the pasta machine on the largest setting or roll by hand to create a narrow strip. Roll the strip thinner and longer until it is approximately 1 mm (1/32 in) thick. If using a pasta machine you will need to find the appropriate setting.

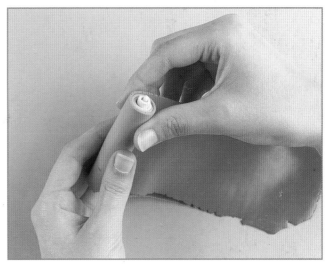

3 Starting at the white end of the blend, roll the strip into a spiral to form a cane with a white middle, fading to red on the outer edge. Let the cane rest then reduce it by squeezing and rolling until the diameter is approximately ¼–⅓ the diameter of the aperture in the card blank. I have used a card blank with an aperture of approximately 8 cm (3⅛ in) so my cane was reduced to a diameter of 1.5 cm (⅝ in).

4 Use a combination of pinching and flattening with your fingertips to shape the reduced cane so that the cross section becomes more oval or petal shaped. Allow the cane to rest then cut several 2 mm (³⁄₃₂ in) slices. Refine the shape of each "petal" by hand and if you wish roll the slices carefully by hand or run through the pasta machine to ensure they are smooth and flat.

5 Roll a 1 mm (¹⁄₃₂ in) sheet of scrap clay and cut a small circle using a round canapé cutter. The circle should be large enough to accommodate the magnet; I used a cutter of 2.5 cm (1 in) diameter. Place the scrap clay circle on to a ceramic tile and position the cane slice "petals" around the edge as shown, pushing them down lightly to adhere to the clay base.

6 Roll a ball of yellow clay large enough to sit in the middle of the petals. Push down with your palm on the ball to flatten it slightly into a dome shape and indent small dots using end of a wooden skewer or ball stylus tool. Place over the center of the petals and push down lightly to adhere to the clay below.

7 Leave the flower in place on the ceramic tile and bake according to the clay manufacturer's instructions. Allow to cool. Attach the magnet to the scrap clay circle on the back of the flower using epoxy two-part glue and allow the glue to set completely. Epoxy glue can be an irritant, take care when using it not to get any on your skin, or better still — wear gloves.

8 Place a small square of double-sided adhesive tape on to the magnet and secure the flower in place inside the card so it peeps through the aperture. Your card is ready for any special birthday or celebration. After the celebration, the magnet can be removed carefully from the card and used to brighten refrigerator doors, the sides of filing cabinets or other metal surfaces.

Variation: **Christmas cards**

A green and white blended cane makes perfect leaves for a Christmas tree, simply arrange slices on to a triangle-shaped base and decorate with a bow and little balls of clay as mini lights. A yellow and green blended cane makes ideal holly leaves to finish the Christmas pudding card perfectly.

Wine Glass Charmers

You put down your wine glass at a party. The problem is so does everyone else – so which glass was yours? With these beautiful wine glass charmers each guest can find their own glass in an instant. Simple canework techniques make mouthwatering citrus fruits, elegantly teamed with silver beads. They are sure to be a talking point at your next dinner party!

Skill level
✳ ✳ ✳

Artist's tip

Remember to remove the charmers before washing the wine glasses, as water will tarnish the metal beads and wire.

You will need

* ❋ I block translucent polymer clay, plus a pinch each of red, yellow, orange and green polymer clay to color
* ❋ I block white polymer clay
* ❋ ½ block yellow polymer clay
* ❋ ¼ block bright green polymer clay
* ❋ ¼ block orange polymer clay
* ❋ ⅛ block emerald green polymer clay
* ❋ Pasta machine or hand roller
* ❋ Tissue blade
* ❋ Wooden toothpick or needle tool
* ❋ Wet/dry sandpaper
* ❋ 8 silver jump rings, 5 mm (³⁄₁₆ in) in diameter
* ❋ Small jewellers' pliers
* ❋ 4 silver colored wine glass charmer loops
* ❋ 20 silver beads, 3 mm (⅛ in) in diameter

1 Divide the translucent clay into four equal sections. Lightly color each section to make clay for the insides of the canes, making a lime green, yellow, orange and pink section. When each section is completely blended, form it into a 15 mm (⅝ in) diameter log and pinch along the length, making it triangular-shaped.

2 Wrap each triangular log with a 1 mm (¹⁄₃₂ in) sheet of white clay. Cut where the clay overlaps and butt the edges together neatly; remember that any overlaps in this white layer will adversely affect the pattern of the cane later. Cut each log into six equal parts and assemble into a circle, again taking care to position all the points together precisely.

3 Finish each cane by wrapping it in a 2 mm (³⁄₃₂ in) thick sheet of colored clay, forming the fruit "skin". Wrap the pink cane with yellow clay to make the ruby grapefruit cane as shown. Wrap the other canes with yellow, bright green and orange creating lemon, lime and orange canes. Allow the canes to rest until they are firm and cool.

4 Reduce the canes, squeezing and rolling them thinner until they reach a diameter of 2 cm (¾ in). Cut a 3 mm (¹⁄₈ in) slice from each cane and pierce a hole at the top for hanging using a wooden toothpick or needle tool. Save the remainder of the canes to use in other projects.

5 Roll 6 mm (¼ in) diameter balls from bright green and emerald green clay. Shape each ball into a pear shape and then flatten to form a leaf, making one for each charmer. Pierce a hole at the top and add vein marks by indenting with the edge of the wooden toothpick or needle tool. Bake all the cane slices and leaves according to the clay manufacturer's instructions. When cool, wet-sand the cane slices smooth.

6 Open the jump rings with a pair of pliers and attach one to each cane slice and leaf, closing them again afterwards. Take care to twist the jump rings open and closed rather than pulling them apart. You may find it easier to use a pair of pliers in each hand to get a firm grip on either side of the jump ring when doing this.

7 Thread the beads, cane slices and leaves on to the wine charmer loops as shown. When all the beads have been threaded, use the pliers to bend up the last 3 mm (⅛ in) of the wire into a 90 degree angle. This will stop the beads falling off and also form a catch, linking into the eyelet on the charmer loop to keep it closed. Open the charmers and place one around the stem of each wine glass, linking it closed again when in place.

Variation: **Charm Bracelet**

Use the remainder of the canes from this project to make a charm bracelet. Attach cane slices to a length of chain and finish with a clasp.

Geometric Filigree Barrette

The filigree technique in polymer clay uses long strings of clay spiralled up to decorate anything from vessels to beads. This project adapts the technique slightly allowing you to create a collage of filigree patterned pieces of clay fitted together to form a geometric design – perfect for pretty hair ornaments. The instructions here are for just one design but once you have started working with filigree, you will be inspired to create your own variations. Use a soft clay for the strings and condition well.

Skill level
✳ ✳ ✳

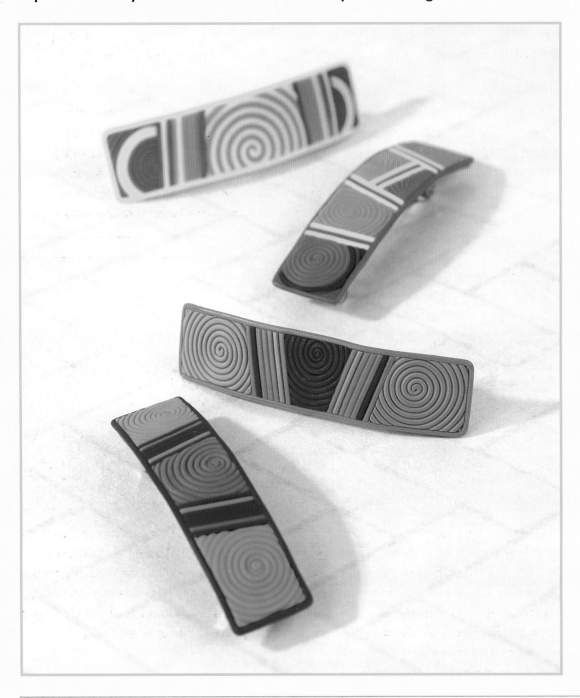

You will need

* ❋ 1 block scrap polymer clay
* ❋ ¼ block pink polymer clay
* ❋ ¼ block turquoise polymer clay
* ❋ ¼ block blue polymer clay
* ❋ Barrette finding
* ❋ Pasta machine or hand roller
* ❋ Clay gun
* ❋ Craft knife
* ❋ Tissue blade
* ❋ Wet/dry sandpaper in 600 and 1200 grits
* ❋ Epoxy two-part glue

1 Roll half the scrap clay into a sheet approximately 1 mm (⅟₃₂ in) thick. Using the clay gun fitted with the 7 hole die, extrude strings of clay from all the colored clays. Clean the barrel of the clay gun between colors by removing the screw-on cap and die and pushing some scrunched up paper towel through the barrel with the plunger.

2 Spiral a string of turquoise clay on to the scrap clay. Push down gently as you wind the clay around to ensure the clay string sticks to the base layer. Repeat to create another turquoise spiral and a blue spiral each approximately 4 cm (1½ in) diameter. Form a 10 cm (4 in) strip using rows of pink clay strings interspaced with lines of the other colors as shown. Carefully cut out the filigree sections using a craft knife.

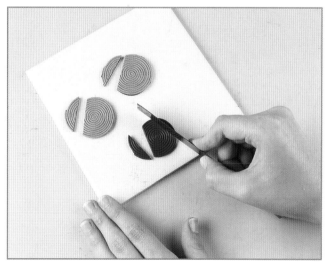

3 Cut a small diagonal piece away from the edge on both turquoise spirals. On the blue spiral, cut away two sections as shown. Cut the lined clay section in half. The cuts on the circles need not be accurate, but ensure the cut is far enough into the circle to give you at least a 2.5 cm (1 in) cut edge.

4 Roll another 1 mm (¹⁄₃₂ in) sheet of scrap clay. Position the cut out pieces on to the clay as shown and press down gently to ensure they have stuck to the clay sheet below. Try to butt the cut edges of the different clay pieces as close together as possible to avoid any gaps.

5 Use either a tissue blade or a metal ruler and craft knife to cut out a rectangle 2 x 9 cm (¾ x 3½ in) from the patterned clay. Take care that you cut only the clay covered with the filigree pattern and do not include any gaps around the top and bottom of the patterned pieces. You can fill any awkward gaps that might be there with the sections you cut away from the spirals in step 3 if necessary.

6 Edge the rectangle with a string of pink clay. Push it gently on to the side of the clay working around the rectangle. Gentle pressure should be sufficient for the clay string to stick to the side of the clay. Cut the string when it meets the beginning edge and smooth the seam gently with your finger. Dipping your finger into a little water and then stroking the clay can make smoothing the seam easier.

Artist's tip

Twist together two logs of different colored clays and load into the clay gun to create marbled strings of clay

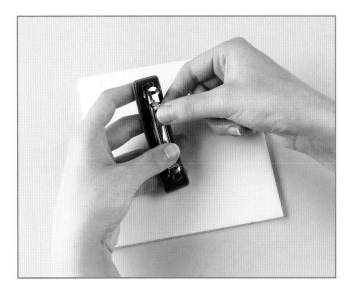

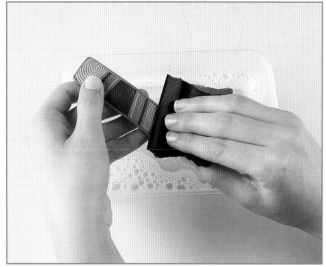

7 Carefully position the clay on to the barrette finding. Place upright on a baking sheet or ceramic tile and bake according to the clay manufacturer's recommendations. Baking on the barrette finding will give the clay the correct curved shape. Be sure to allow the clay to cool completely before you remove it from the barrette. Baked clay is still very pliable when fresh from the oven and the clay must cool in position on the barrette to retain the correct shape.

8 Once the clay is cool, wet-sand lightly with some 600 and then 1200 grit sandpaper. Glue the barrette finding in place using some epoxy two-part glue. The barrette can be left with a matt finish, buffed to a high sheen or given a coat of varnish.

Variation: Antiqued Filigree Barrette

The antiquing technique can also be used to highlight the filigree pattern. Simply coat the barrette with a thin wash of dark brown acrylic paint and either wipe back when wet or allow the paint to dry and then sand back.

Further Inspiration: Combining Ideas

 Mixing different ideas and techniques together is an excellent way to devise new projects, giving you endless possibilities.

The picture frame and journals combine different polymer clay techniques together to decorate non-clay items. The picture frame project uses molding and antiquing methods to decorate a basic wooden frame. The frame was coated with PVA glue and covered with sections of white clay shaped using simple molds. Small balls of clay were used to fill the gaps between the molded sections and pushed into place with a ball stylus. Once baked, the clay was covered with blue acrylic paint and wiped back to highlight the detail. The plain artists' journals were jazzed up with flat decorations made from black clay brushed with colored mica powders. The decorations were baked, varnished and then attached to the book covers using PVA glue.

The "Chevron" decorated mirrors combine standard and liquid polymer clay with other embellishments. A section of mirror glass was laid on to a base sheet of scrap clay that had been cut a little larger than the mirror. Sections of clay were built up around and slightly overlapping the glass to form a secure frame, leaving a small channel along each side to hold the liquid polymer clay. Glass nuggets and semi precious stones were embedded into the corners for decoration and the clay then covered with pewter-colored bronze powder. The channel in the frame was carefully filled with drops of liquid polymer clay, pre-colored by mixing with different mica powders, and a pin dragged through the liquid clay to give the feathering effects. Once baked, the clay was varnished and a hook glued to the back for hanging.

The *cloisonné* style boxes were constructed from scrap clay in the same way as the Millefiore Trinket Box project (see page 43). Thin clay strings were positioned on the lid to create the outline of the flower motifs and all the clay was brushed over with gold-colored bronze powder. The cells formed by the outline were filled with colored liquid polymer clay then baked and varnished to finish.

Apples and Bugs Mobile

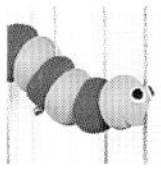

This fun mobile project will brighten up any room from the nursery to the kitchen. The hungry caterpillars are surprisingly simple to make, using only the most basic modelling techniques, while the colorful apples are given a ripe and rosy glow with Skinner blends.

Skill level

You will need

- 1½ blocks pale green polymer clay
- 1½ blocks pink polymer clay
- 1 block red polymer clay
- 1 block yellow polymer clay
- 1 block pale blue polymer clay
- ⅛ block white polymer clay
- Pinch of black polymer clay
- Tissue blade
- Hand roller or pasta machine
- Guide rods
- Apple shaped cookie cutter, 7 cm (2¾ in) in diameter
- Wooden toothpick or needle tool
- Fluted round cookie cutter, 4 cm (1½ in) in diameter
- Metal bowl, 570 ml (1 pint) capacity
- Wet/dry sandpaper
- Pale blue embroidery yarn
- A small brass curtain ring
- Superglue
- 8 paperclips

Artist's tip

You can use many different cookie cutters to make attractive mobiles; sheets of marbled clay cut with a butterfly-shaped cutter would work well

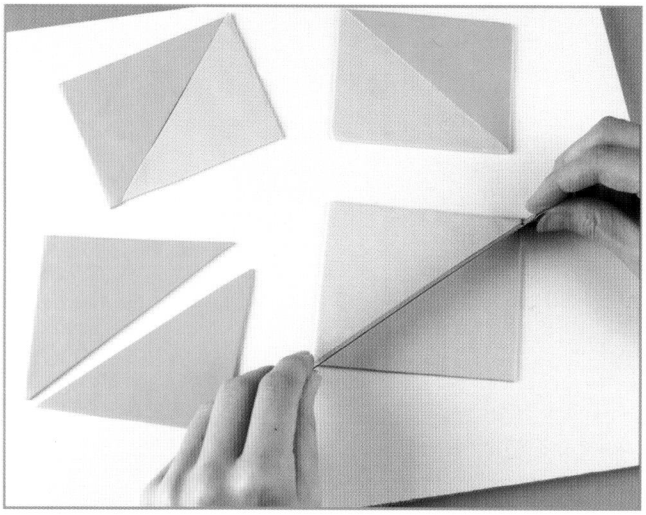

1 Divide the pink and the green clay each into two equal sections and roll each one into a 3 mm (⅛ in) thick sheet. Trim each sheet to form a rectangle just large enough to accommodate the cookie cutter and then cut diagonally, forming two right-angled triangles. Pair up different color triangles as shown, making four rectangles ready for blending.

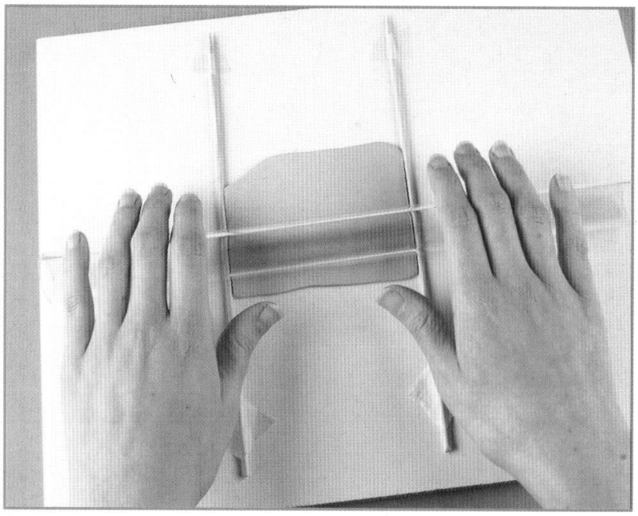

2 Take each of the rectangles in turn and form into a Skinner blend 3 mm (⅛ in) thick (see page 19). The Skinner blends should still be only as wide as the cookie cutter. Rather than using a pasta machine, which tends to widen the blend, you may find it easier to roll the blends by hand. Roll using guide rods taped to the work surface at the correct distance apart.

3 Use the cookie cutter to cut an apple shape from each blended sheet. Pierce a hole in the top of each apple for hanging, using a wooden toothpick or needle tool. Cut a "bite" mark into the side of two of the apples using the edge of the fluted cookie cutter. Leave the other two apples whole. When complete, set the apples aside on a lined baking sheet.

Artist's tip

Dust the cutters lightly with talcum powder or cornstarch to prevent them sticking to the clay

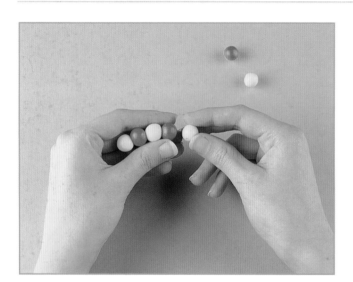

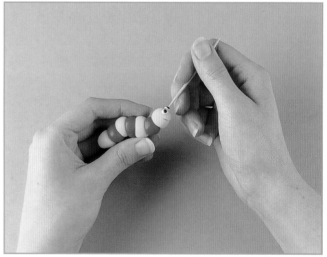

4 Roll four balls of yellow clay and three of red, each 12 mm (½ in) in diameter. Starting with yellow gently push the balls together in a line, alternating the colors, to form the body of the caterpillar. Shape the body into a slight "S" shape. Repeat to make four caterpillar bodies in total.

5 To give each caterpillar a mouth, cut a small slit with a tissue blade and open it up slightly. Roll tiny balls of white and black clay to make the eyes and poke these firmly into place with a wooden toothpick. Pierce a hole through the middle red section of each caterpillar then set them aside on the baking sheet.

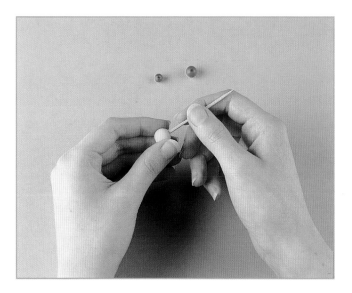

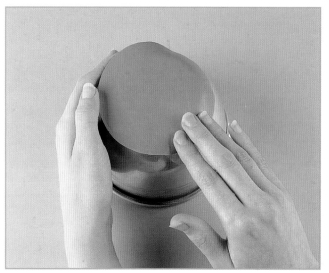

6 Make the beads for the mobile's hanger. Roll two red clay balls, 5 mm (³⁄₁₆ in) and 8 mm (⁵⁄₁₆ in) in diameter. Using yellow clay, roll a 12 mm (½ in) diameter ball. Pierce all the beads and set them aside on the lined baking sheet.

7 Roll the pale blue clay into a sheet 3 mm (⅛ in) thick. Cut out a circle, roughly 3 cm (1¼ in) larger in diameter than the bottom of the metal bowl. Use a cup, lid or saucer of the right size as a template and wash well after use to remove any clay residue. Place the clay over the up-turned metal bowl and smooth down to create the dome.

8 Pierce a small hole in the center of the clay dome. Pierce eight holes around the side equally distanced and at least 5 mm (³⁄₁₆ in) away from the edge. Keeping the clay on the bowl, bake along with other clay pieces according to the clay manufacturer's instructions. When cool, wet-sand the apples and dome to a smooth finish.

9 Thread a length of embroidery yarn through the curtain ring, then thread both ends through the larger red bead and the yellow bead. Thread both ends through the central hole in the dome and finally thread on the small red bead. Pull the two ends taut and knot them together, making sure the knot cannot pass through the bead. Secure the knot by dabbing on a drop of superglue and cut away the loose ends.

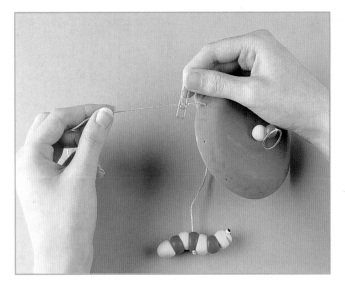

10 Cut another length of yarn and knot it at the bottom. Thread on a caterpillar, checking it cannot pass over the knot. Secure the knot with superglue and cut away the loose ends. Thread the other end of the yarn through one of the side holes in the clay dome, threading from the inside of the dome outwards, and secure temporarily with a paperclip.

11 Thread another length of yarn through the hanging hole in one of the apples. Tie a knot, fixing the apple to the bottom of the yarn, then secure the knot with superglue and cut away the loose ends. Thread the other end through the next side hole in the clay dome. As before, secure the thread temporarily with a paperclip.

12 Continue adding caterpillars and apples around the mobile. When complete, experiment with the lengths of the different yarns until you are happy with the positioning of each. Knot each yarn back around itself securely then remove the paperclip and cut away the loose ends. Slide the knots to the back of the clay dome out of sight. Using a small drop of superglue, attach each knot securely to the back surface of the clay dome.

Safety tip

Take great care when using superglues, they can bond your skin to anything and everything in seconds!

Millefiore Trinket Box

These pretty trinket boxes are wonderful for hiding away little odds and ends and they make great gifts too! Using metal cookie cutters as a form, you can soon create boxes in all shapes and sizes. They are easy to make and a superb way to use up those small sections of millefiore canes left over from other projects.

Skill level
✳ ✳ ✳

You will need

* ❋ I block pink polymer clay
* ❋ ½ block bright green clay
* ❋ Several different millefiore canes, reduced to I cm (⅜ in) in diameter (see pages 16–18)
* ❋ Pasta machine or hand roller
* ❋ Metal heart shaped cookie cutter, 5 cm (2 in) diameter
* ❋ Tissue blade
* ❋ Ceramic tiles
* ❋ Craft knife
* ❋ Clay gun (optional)
* ❋ Liquid polymer clay
* ❋ Wet/dry sandpaper
* ❋ Paintbrush and varnish

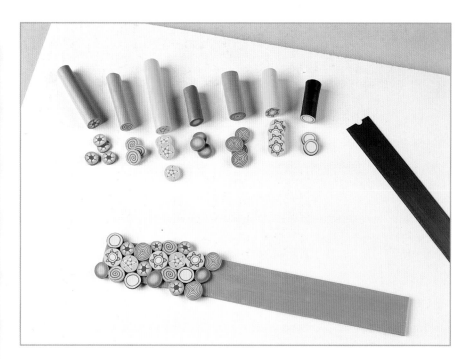

I Roll a strip of pink clay 2 mm (³⁄₃₂ in) thick. Make it long enough to wrap around the cookie cutter and I cm (⅜ in) wider than the cutter is tall. Cut thin slices from the canes and arrange them on the clay strip. When completely covered, roll the strip by hand or with a pasta machine to smooth out the seams between the cane slices. Trim the edges to neaten.

2 Wrap the clay strip around the cookie cutter. Where the clay overlaps, trim away the excess and butt the cut edges together. Trim the clay in line with the top and bottom edge of the cutter. Place on to a ceramic tile or lined baking tray and bake according to the clay manufacturer's instructions. Allow the baked clay to cool completely then carefully remove from the cutter.

Artist's tip

Carefully run a craft knife around the inside edge of the baked clay to loosen it from the cutter

3 To make the box lid roll a 2 mm (³⁄₃₂ in) thick sheet of pink clay, making it a little larger than the area of the wall section already made. Cover the sheet with cane slices and roll smooth. Place the sheet upside down on to a ceramic tile. Place the wall section on the sheet and cut around the outside edge with a craft knife.

Artist's tip

Hold the craft knife as upright as possible when cutting for a neat finish

4 Roll a 3 mm (¹⁄₈ in) sheet of bright green clay and lay the wall section on the surface. Cut around the inside edge to make a flange for the box lid. Carefully lift the flange and position on the back of the lid, ensuring it is placed in the middle. When you are happy that the positioning is correct push it down gently to adhere.

5 To finish the lid, form a pink clay string either by hand or using a clay gun. Place the string around the outer edge of the box lid, pushing it gently to adhere. Cut where the string overlaps and butt the two edges together. Smooth the seam with your fingertip.

6 To make the base, roll a 2 mm (³⁄₃₂ in) square of pink clay and place on a ceramic tile. Dab a little liquid polymer clay around the bottom edge of the wall section and position onto the clay sheet. Cut around the outside with a craft knife and remove the excess clay, this time keeping the wall section in place when you have finished.

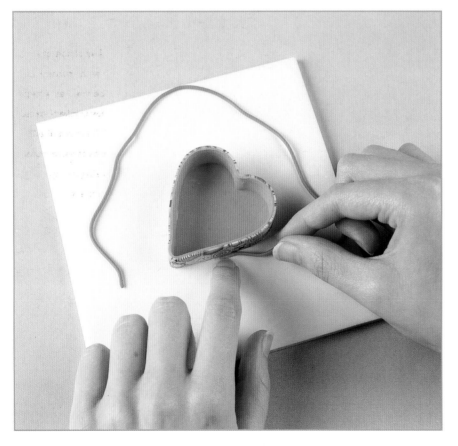

7 Roll another pink clay string and place around the base of the box, to hide the cut edge. Leave both parts of the trinket box in place on their ceramic tiles and bake according to the clay manufacturer's instructions. Allow all the pieces to cool completely before removing from the tiles.

Artist's tip

Beware of pushing the wall section out of place as you are working. The liquid polymer clay will not actually stick the clay pieces together until it is baked

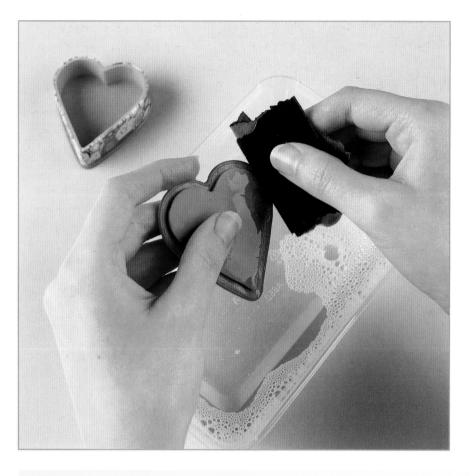

8 Wet-sand all visible surfaces well using wet/dry sandpaper. Start with 600 grit then use higher grit paper until the box is smooth. Check that the lid fits the box and if necessary sand the edge of the flange to make any adjustments. Finish with two coats of varnish.

Artist's tip

After wet–sanding, make
sure the clay is completely
dry before varnishing

Variation: **Pill boxes**

Any shape of metal cutter can be used as a form for trinket boxes. These small pill boxes were made using canapé cutters.

Fluorite Mokume Egg

Eggs are a symbol of life and fertility, so giving decorative eggs is traditional to many cultures all over the world. This project is inspired by the ever-popular, polished stone eggs. Colored translucent clays mimicking the look of fluorite are given the Mokume Gane treatment, creating a beautiful egg formed around a real eggshell.

Artist's tip

Use free–range eggs – they are not only kinder, but have stronger shells!

You will need

* ❈ I large free-range egg
* ❈ I block scrap polymer clay
* ❈ ½ block translucent polymer clay
* ❈ ½ block green-colored translucent polymer clay
* ❈ ½ block violet-colored translucent polymer clay
* ❈ Darning needle
* ❈ Bowl
* ❈ Pasta machine or hand roller
* ❈ Non-flammable polyester batting or wadding (available from fabric, craft stores)
* ❈ Tissue blade
* ❈ Silver-colored decorative metal leaf
* ❈ Wet/dry sandpaper in 600 and 1200 grit.
* ❈ Paintbrush and varnish

1. Wash and dry the egg and then pierce a hole in the top and bottom of the egg with the needle. Poke the needle into the egg to break the yolk and, with your mouth covering the top hole, blow the contents of the egg into a bowl. When empty, rinse the eggshell thoroughly and bake in a low oven for 10 minutes to dry the inside.

2. Roll the scrap clay into a sheet I mm (¹⁄₃₂ in) thick. Fold the sheet around the eggshell pinching the clay together tightly. Trim away the excess clay and smooth the seam. Pierce through the clay covering the hole in the bottom in the eggshell. This will allow air to escape when the egg is baked. Support the egg on some polyester batting placed on a baking sheet and bake according to the clay manufacturer's instructions.

3. Roll the colored and plain translucent clays into 15 mm (⅝ in) diameter logs. Twist the logs together then roll and fold again, repeating a few times to marble the clays. Do not let the clay become too blended, stop marbling while you can still see bands of individual colors.

4 Cut away about a fifth of the marbled clay log and set aside. Roll the remainder of the clay into a 1 mm (1/32 in) thick sheet. Cut two squares from the sheet, the same size as the decorative metal leaf. Carefully place each square on to a sheet of metal leaf and lift up. Smooth the leaf on to the clay with a soft brush.

5 Cut the squares into quarters and stack the pieces, leaf side up, to form a slab. Cover the top of the slab with a 1 mm (1/32 in) sheet made from the clay set aside earlier. With the leftover clay, roll several 15 mm (5/8 in) diameter balls. Position these on to the clay stack, leaving space around each one. Turn the stack over and push down around the balls, forming hills and valleys in the clay surface.

6 Holding a tissue blade horizontally, take thin slices from the top of each mound. As you cut, the circular pattern will emerge. The first few slices are usually the most defined, so set these aside to be used last. Keep cutting thin layers from the slab, the slices will become larger with more random patterns as you continue.

7 Cover the egg with the Mokume Gane slices. Start with the larger slices taken last from the slab and push these on to the egg. When the egg is covered with these, use the more decorative slices, cut first, to add detail. Try to apply the slices evenly, creating a layer of equal thickness all around the egg.

8 Smooth the egg by rolling between your palms or gently rolling with a brayer. The smoother you can get the clay now, the less sanding later! If the clay becomes too soft, let the egg rest and continue when the clay is firmer. Pierce through the clay covering the air hole and bake according to the clay manufacturer's instructions. When cool, wet-sand the egg and then varnish.

Artist's tip

When varnishing, support the egg on a needle tool inserted into the air hole.

Variation: Mokume Gane Pendants

Use the remainder of the Mokume Gane slabs to make attractive beads and pendants.

Metallic Napkin Rings

 Add contemporary sparkle to your dinner table with these glittering napkin rings. With PVC piping providing the base, they are durable as well as attractive. I have used glitter type metallic clays in this project, but any type of metallic clay will give equally nice results. The clay amounts specified are enough to make at least four napkin rings, adjust the quantities if you wish to make a different number.

Artist's tip

Larger diameter PVC pipe can be used to make bangle type bracelets using the same methods.

Skill level
✳ ✳ ✳

You will need

- ❋ 1 block silver metallic polymer clay
- ❋ 1 block gold metallic polymer clay
- ❋ 1 block anthracite metallic polymer clay
- ❋ 1 block scrap polymer clay
- ❋ 5 cm (2 in) diameter PVC pipe, allow 3 cm (1¼ in) per napkin ring
- ❋ Metal ruler
- ❋ Bench vice
- ❋ Small hacksaw
- ❋ Wet/dry sandpaper 400 grit
- ❋ Pasta machine or hand roller
- ❋ Gold-colored and silver-colored decorative metal leaf
- ❋ Tissue blade
- ❋ Craft knife
- ❋ PVA glue
- ❋ 1 mm diameter (18-gauge) copper wire, allow 8 cm (3⅛ in) per napkin ring
- ❋ Small jewellers' pliers
- ❋ Wire cutters
- ❋ Superglue
- ❋ Paintbrush and varnish

1 Mark along the PVC pipe at 3 cm (1¼ in) intervals, measuring out a base section for each napkin ring. Fit the pipe into a bench vice and cut off each section using a small hacksaw. Wet-sand the cut edges smooth and roughen the outside of the pipe, using 400 grit wet/dry sandpaper.

2 Cut each metallic clay block in half. Roll one section of each color into 1 mm (½₂ in) thick sheets and set aside. Roll the remaining sections into sheets 2 mm (³⁄₃₂ in) thick. Cover the 2 mm (³⁄₃₂ in) sheets with decorative metal leaf and roll each thinner until it is 1 mm (½₂ in) thick and the metal leaf has crackled. I placed gold-colored leaf on the silver clay and silver-colored leaf on the other colors.

3 Roll a 1 mm (⅟₃₂ in) thick strip of scrap polymer clay, long enough to wrap around the PVC pipe and 5 cm (2 in) wide. Cut random sections from the different clay sheets and arrange on the scrap clay base as shown. When the strip is completely covered, roll gently with a hand roller to smooth the seams between the clay pieces.

Artist's tip

Sections of clay can also be laid diagonally or horizontally for a different look

4 Coat a section of PVC pipe with a thin layer of PVA glue. Allow the glue to dry and then wrap the patterned clay around the pipe. Cut the clay strip where it overlaps, removing any excess clay. Butt the cut edges together neatly and roll the pipe gently along the work surface to smooth the seam.

5 Smooth the edges of the clay over towards the inside of the PVC pipe. Gently roll across the sides of the pipe with the hand roller, just enough to flatten each edge. Trim away the excess clay with a craft knife, cutting flush to the inside of the pipe.

6 Cut an 8 cm (3⅛ in) section of copper wire. Bend the first 5 mm (³⁄₁₆ in) down into a right angle using a pair of pliers. This will provide an end to be embedded into the clay. Hold this securely in the jaws of the pliers and spiral the remaining wire around, making an open coil shape. Make another right angle bend in the tail end of the wire and then trim both ends to 1.5 mm (⅟₁₆ in) long.

Artist's tip

Wrap the jaws of the pliers with masking tape to prevent them scratching the wire as you work

7 Choose an area of the napkin ring to make into the focal point and push the copper spiral into the clay. Repeat the above instructions to make another three napkin rings. When finished place them on to a lined baking tray and bake according to the clay manufacturer's instructions.

8 Allow the baked napkin rings to cool completely before handling as they can easily be pushed out of shape while warm. When cool, check that the copper coils are secure in the clay. If any are loose remove them and glue back in place using a drop of superglue. Give each napkin ring several coats of varnish to protect the decorative metal leaf, allowing each coat to dry thoroughly.

Plant Pot Critters

Simple sculpture and millefiore cane making techniques are used in this project to make fun adornments for your house plants. This little turtle will be perfectly at home among the foliage and by adapting the techniques many other animals can be created too, forming your own mini menagerie!

Artist's tip

Other shell dwelling critters can be made in the same way. Adapt the project to make a crab for example. Different creatures can also be made by combining very basic ball and log shaped sections of clay and simple sculpting techniques.

Skill level
✳ ✳ ✳

You will need

* 1 block beige polymer clay
* ¼ block yellow polymer clay
* ⅛ block green polymer clay
* ¼ block brown polymer clay
* Craft knife
* Wooden toothpick or needle tool
* Pasta machine or hand roller
* Clay gun (optional)
* Wooden barbecue skewer
* 600 grit sandpaper
* Acrylic paints
* Superglue

1 Using the beige clay, roll a 20 mm (¾ in) ball. Flatten this gently to make the body. Roll four 10 mm (⅜ in) balls and one 12 mm (½ in) ball to make the head. Roll each of the balls into a slight cone shape. Push the narrow side of the cones on to the body to form the head and limbs as shown. Roll a small log, taper one end to make a tail and push into place.

2 Pinch the head between your thumb and forefinger to give the turtle a pointed face. Using a craft knife, cut a slit into the clay and open slightly to make a mouth. Roll two tiny balls of brown clay to make eyes and push into place. Use a fingertip to flatten the limbs slightly to create flippers, add markings by pressing the edge of a wooden toothpick gently on to the clay surface as shown.

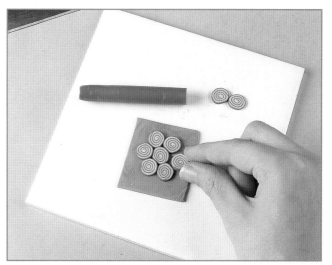

3 Roll a 2 mm (³⁄₃₂ in) strip from the yellow clay and a 1 mm (¹⁄₃₂ inch) strip from the green clay and form into a spiral cane. Reduce the cane to a diameter of 10 mm (⅜ in.) Roll a small sheet of scrap clay and cover with slices from the cane as shown. Roll the sheet thinner to about 1.5 mm (¹⁄₁₆ in) thick so that the sheet is smooth and the seams between the cane slices have disappeared.

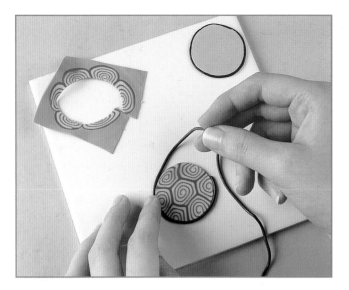

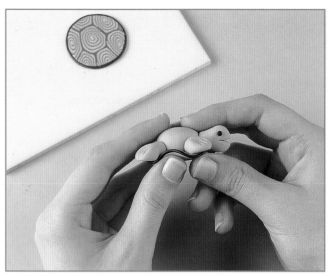

4 Roll a 1.5 mm (¹⁄₁₆ in) sheet of beige clay and cut a circle approximately 35 mm (1¼ in) in diameter. Edge the circle with a small string of brown clay, pushing it to the side with your fingertips. Where the string overlaps, trim and smooth away the seam. Cut and edge a matching circle from the sheet covered with cane slices. These circles will form the top and bottom of the turtle's shell.

5 Place the turtle body on to the center of the beige circle and carefully push the outer edge of the circle up around the body so it loosely hugs the limbs, head and tail. Push the sheet up slightly in between the gaps between the legs, head and tail but use a light pressure to maintain the general rounded shape of a turtle shell, with no harsh angles.

6 Place the patterned circle of clay on the top of the turtle's body and push down gently around the edge, encasing the body in the "shell" so only the legs, head and tail peek out. Twist the end of the skewer halfway up into the underside of the body to make a hole. Remover the skewer and bake the turtle according to the clay manufacturer's instructions. Allow to cool then sand and varnish if you wish.

7 Sand the wooden skewer smooth with 600 grit sandpaper. Paint with two coats of acrylic paint. When the paint is dry cut off the top end of the skewer to leave a length of 15 cm (6 in) from the pointed end to the cut end. The skewers can be cut using a pair of heavy-duty scissors. It is advisable to wear eye protection when cutting the skewer. Glue the turtle in place on the stick using a drop of superglue.

Clay and Metal Earrings

 **These metallic earrings are wafer thin without being fragile. The clay is given a unique decoration and then laminated on to thin aluminum sheet. Usually used for embossing work, this fine metal sheet gives strength and form to the earrings – proving that polymer clay jewelery does not have to be chunky.**

Artist's tip

Countless styles of earrings can be made using this technique. Cut around different canapé cutters and curve the metal over the side of a small bottle for other interesting shapes.

Skill level
✳ ✳ ✳

You will need

- ✻ ¼ block scrap polymer clay
- ✻ Pasta machine or hand roller
- ✻ Ceramic tile
- ✻ Rubber stamps or wooden printing blocks
- ✻ Gold-colored bronze powder
- ✻ Soft brush
- ✻ Acrylic paints in metallic colors
- ✻ Paint brush
- ✻ 3 cm (1¼ in) round canapé cutter
- ✻ Needle tool or sharp dental pick
- ✻ Gold-colored aluminum sheet, 0.15 mm (.006 in) thick
- ✻ Scissors
- ✻ Large knitting needle
- ✻ PVA glue
- ✻ Varnish
- ✻ Pair of gold earring findings

1 Roll the scrap clay into a 1 mm (⅟₃₂ in) thick sheet and place on to a ceramic tile. Use rubber stamps or wooden printing blocks to impress texture on to the clay. Make the impressions quite deep and create repeating patterns as you will need to cut two similar sections from the clay to form the pair of earrings.

2 Brush gold-colored bronze powder over the entire sheet. Work the powder into all the crevices of the texture using a soft brush. When complete, brush the sheet gently to remove any loose powder. Remember to wear a face mask when using the bronze powders to prevent inhaling the metal particles.

Safety

Always use a protective face mask when using colored bronze powders.

3 Mix up different colors of metallic acrylic paints, adding water until the paints have the consistency of milk. Use a paintbrush to dab a generous amount of one color on to the sheet. Dab different areas with drops of other colors, letting the colors bleed together. The powder will act as a resist and the paint will settle into the hollows of the texture.

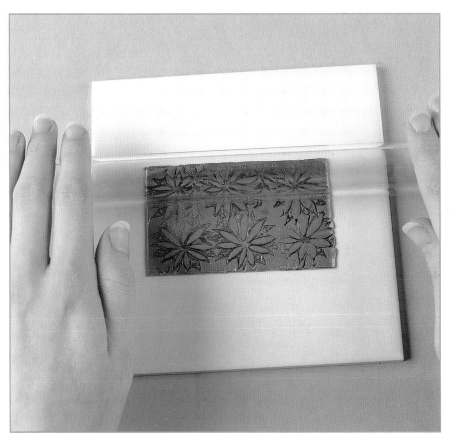

4 Leave the clay in place on the ceramic tile and let the paint dry completely – this will take a couple of hours. Make sure you keep the tile level or the paint will drain to one side. When dry, roll the clay with a hand roller just enough to smooth out the texture.

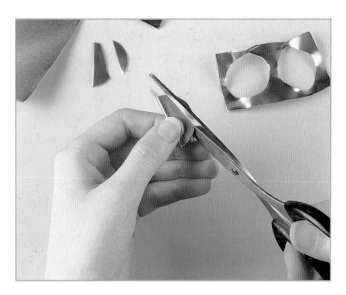

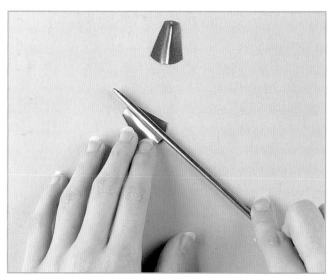

5 Scoring around the canapé cutter with a needle tool, mark out two circles on the aluminum sheet. Cut out the circles with a pair of scissors and fold each one in half. Cut diagonal sections away from the metal shapes as shown, cutting the first by eye and then using this as a template to cut the second shape.

6 Unfold both metal circles. The raised ridge left where the metal was folded provides form for the finished earring. Place the metal shapes on a firm work surface and, without flattening out these ridges, burnish the rest of the metal flat, smoothing it with the side of a large knitting needle. Take care not to cut your fingers on the metal edges.

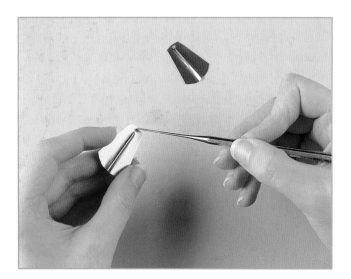

7 Use the knitting needle to flatten down the top 3 mm (⅛ in) of the ridge. In this space, pierce a hole 1.5 mm (¹⁄₁₆ in) away from the edge using a needle tool or sharp toothpick. Turn the metal shape over and flatten away any sharp edges around the hole, taking care not to flatten out the rest of the ridge against the work surface.

8 Cut two matching rectangles from the clay sheet large enough to cover the metal shapes. Depending on the patterns used and the random nature of the paint effects you may not find two identical sections. If so, select areas that will make a nice co-ordinating pair. Apply a light coating of PVA glue to the upper side of the metal shapes and allow the glue to dry.

9 Place the metal shapes on to the back of the clay rectangles. Smooth the clay on to the metal by rolling with the edge of the knitting needle, pushing the clay into the curves around the ridge. Use a light and gentle touch while smoothing the clay and avoid touching the patterned surface more than is necessary.

10 Laying the clay face down, trim around the metal shapes with a craft knife. Let the metal shape overhang the edge of a ceramic tile so that the clay covering the raised ridge is not flattened against the work surface. Using a curved blade in the craft knife is helpful as you can roll the cutting edge rather than pulling it through the clay.

11 Smooth down the cut edges with your fingertip. Use a light touch and gently stroke the very edge of the cut clay in downward movements. Work around both shapes until the edges are neat and smooth. Pierce through the clay covering the holes in the metal, to provide hanging holes for the earring findings.

12 Bake the earrings according to the clay manufacturer's instructions. When cool, varnish to protect the metallic powders and paints and let the varnish dry. Attach gold earring findings to complete.

Further Inspiration: Expanding Ideas

These different pieces of jewelery show how you can take a project (in this case the Clay and Metal earrings project) and expand the idea further. By experimenting with ideas in this way you can tailor any technique you learn to suit you, creating your own unique variations.

The blue and pink pendant is a simple adaptation of the original project. A rectangle shape was cut from the metal sheet. It was curved, pierced and covered with decorated clay using the same method as the original earrings project. Once baked, it was finished with wire-work and semi precious bead dangles. The domed sections in the neighbouring necklace were formed by shaping circles cut from the metal sheet in a doming block and then decorating in the same manner. The hair barrette used a larger free-form shaped base. A piece of wooden skewer was painted and capped with a ball of gold-colored clay to create the stick. Metal sheet was cut into a range of simple, flat shapes to make all the other jewelry in that style.

While this project can be adapted easily to make flat or curved components for jewelry, making solid beads is not so simple. But the style and coloration of the clay and metal jewelry can be used to inspire different ideas that fit the theme. The beaded bracelet uses scrap clay sheets, decorated with foils and colored mica powders. Large and small triangle sections cut from the sheets were stacked together and rolled up around a skewer, as if rolling up a croissant from pastry. The ends of these beads were then trimmed and each bead was pinched into a rectangle shape. The pendant was made from the same decorated clay sheets. Shapes cut from the sheets were applied to a flattened ball of scrap clay. The pendant was finished by decorating with more colored mica powders, before being pierced, baked and then varnished.

Multi-Layered Pens

Thin layers of translucent clay embellish this project, transforming disposable ball point pens into magical masterpieces. There are many types of pen you can use; those with opaque barrels usually work well, but avoid clear barrelled pens – they will melt! Before covering a pen for the first time, remove the ink cartridge and test the barrel in the oven to check it can withstand the baking temperature without warping.

Skill level
✳ ✳ ✳

You will need

- ✤ ½ block pink polymer clay
- ✤ ½ block orange polymer clay
- ✤ ½ block translucent polymer clay
- ✤ ¼ block white polymer clay
- ✤ Pinch of turquoise polymer clay
- ✤ Pasta machine or hand roller
- ✤ Suitable disposable ball point pen
- ✤ Tissue blade
- ✤ Pliers
- ✤ Craft knife
- ✤ Gold-colored decorative metal leaf
- ✤ Wet/dry sandpaper in 600 and 1200 grits
- ✤ Paintbrush and varnish

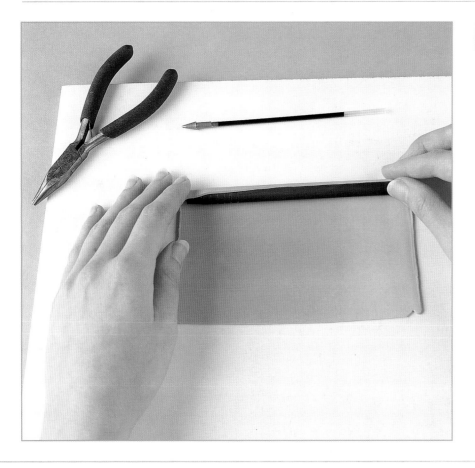

Form a Skinner blend from the pink and orange clay (see page 19). Roll to 1 mm (⅟₃₂ in) thick and cut a section wide enough and long enough to cover the pen. Remove the ink cartridge section from the pen using a pair of pliers and roll the empty pen barrel up in the blended sheet. Where the clay overlaps, trim away the excess and butt the edges together. Smooth the seam and pinch clay over the end of the pen, covering it neatly. Roll the pen along the work surface until it is smooth and even.

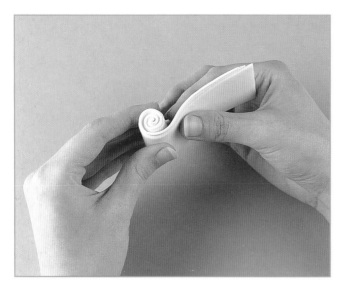

2 Roll half of the translucent clay into a 2 mm (³⁄₃₂ in) thick strip. Cover this with a 1 mm (¹⁄₃₂ in) thick strip of white clay and roll both up together to make a spiral cane. Allow the cane to rest then reduce to a 1 cm (³⁄₈ in) diameter. Cool the cane in the refrigerator after reducing as it will be easier to cut thin slices if the clay is firm.

3 Using a sharp tissue blade, cut a few paper thin slices from the spiral cane and place randomly on the pen. Take great care when using the blade – hold the cane in your hand while cutting and dust the blade with a little talcum powder to reduce drag. When finished, roll the pen along the work surface until the cane slices have sunk in to the background and the clay is smooth.

4 Color the remainder of the translucent clay with a pinch of turquoise colored clay. When completely mixed, roll as thin as possible and cut out a small section. Cover this with gold-colored decorative metal leaf and then fold in half, sandwiching the leaf in the middle. Roll to crackle the leaf, again rolling the clay paper thin. If rolling by hand, dust both sides of the clay with a small amount of talcum powder so the clay does not stick as you roll.

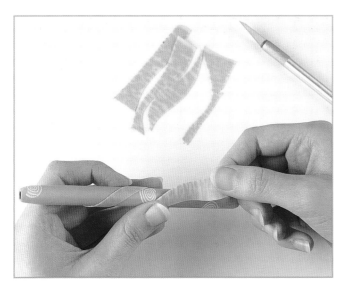

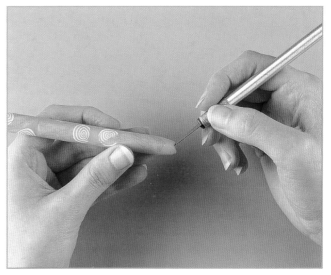

5 Cut random sections from the translucent clay using a craft knife. Curved triangles work very well, but any shapes can be used. Position these sections on the pen, with some points slightly overlapping some of the cane slices already applied. When finished, roll the pen along the work surface to smooth, as before.

6 Cut more paper thin slices from the spiral cane. Apply to the pen, sometimes overlapping slightly the translucent clay already applied. Roll the pen smooth and then trim around the opening where the ink cartridge sits. Place the pen on a lined baking sheet and bake according to the clay manufacturer's instructions.

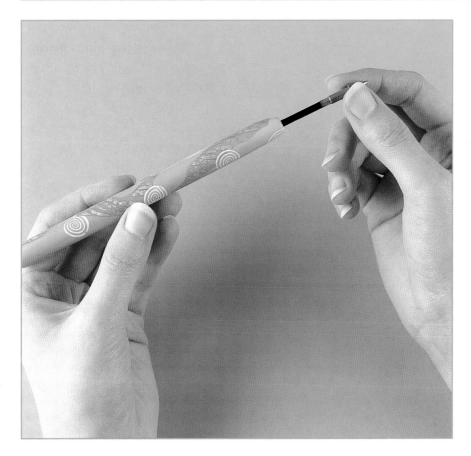

7 When the pen is ready, remove from the oven and plunge straight into a bowl of ice cold water. This technique can help improve the clarity of translucent clays. Wet-sand the pen to an ultra smooth finish starting with 600 grit wet/dry sandpaper and then progressing to a higher grit such as 1200. Apply a coat of varnish and allow to dry. Finally, replace the ink cartridge section. The pen is easily refillable by popping in a new ink cartridge.

Safety tip

Never plunge covered glass items into cold water straight from the oven as the temperature change can cause thermal shock making the glass shatter

Lattice Technique Bowl

There are lots of ways to imitate a lattice or basket weave look in polymer clay. Many involve literally weaving the clay or cutting and positioning tiny pieces. This fluted bowl is made using a much easier process, giving an interesting lattice texture without the hard work! Use a strong clay for making the clay strings, condition well and add clay softener if necessary.

Artist's tip

Save the off–cuts from this project; they will mix together into an emerald green shade that can be used in other projects

Skill level
❋ ❋ ❋

1 Using both blocks of emerald clay, roll a 1 mm (¹⁄₃₂ in) thick base sheet large enough to accommodate the plate. If you are using a pasta machine roll two wide strips and overlap them slightly to join, then roll the seams smooth with a hand roller. Using a clay gun and the 7 hole die, extrude all the other colored clays into long strings and set aside.

2 Lay a string of bright green clay horizontally across the middle of the sheet. Push down slightly and lay more strings above and below, leaving a gap of 5 mm (³⁄₁₆ in) between each. When the sheet is covered, lay a sheet of baking parchment over the top and gently roll with a hand roller. Roll lightly, just enough to flatten the strings slightly and ensure they are securely adhered to the base.

3 Use strings of yellow clay to make the next layer. This time lay a string vertically, again starting in the middle of the sheet. Complete this layer by placing strings to the left and right, leaving the same gap as before. Once the sheet is complete, lay baking parchment over the entire sheet and gently roll.

4 Continue with a third layer using turquoise strings. This layer will be placed horizontally again, but this time, position each string so that it sits in between the first horizontal strings placed. Complete the lattice effect with a fourth and final layer using bright green clay strings laid vertically. After completing each layer, remember to lay the baking parchment on the sheet and roll the surface lightly.

5 Place the plate on top of the lattice sheet and cut around with a craft knife, keeping the blade as upright as possible. Form a thin strip of scrap clay, long enough and tall enough to edge the entire circle. Position the clay strip on the side of the circle so that it hides the cut edge, pushing it gently to adhere. You can either use a clay gun to form the strip or cut one from a long strip of clay.

6 Carefully turn the circle over so you can work on the underside. Brush the underside with gold-colored bronze or mica powder, making sure that you cover the side strip of clay as well as the entire back of the circle. Brush over lightly with a soft brush to remove any loose powder. If you prefer to use acrylic paint, skip this step and paint the base of the bowl after baking.

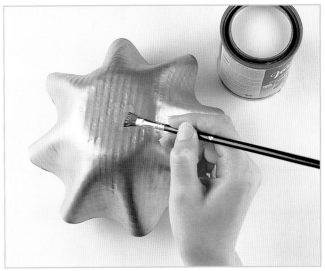

7 Hold the circle in your hand, lattice side uppermost, and place the base of the metal bowl in the middle. Turn the bowl upside down keeping the clay sheet in place as you do so. The clay sheet will now drape over the pudding basin. Gently arrange the folds into a position you are happy with, taking care not to transfer any gold powder from your hands on to the lattice side of the clay.

8 Bake the clay in place on the metal bowl according to the clay manufacturer's instructions and allow to cool completely before removing. Varnish the gold areas of the bowl to protect the powdered surface but leave the inside of the bowl un-varnished. Remember that polymer clay dishes are not suitable for food.

Variation: **Lattice Dish**

This shallow dish shows the very different look that can be achieved by rolling the strings of clay completely flat as you build up the lattice effect.

Safety

Always use a protective face mask when using decorative powders.

Wine Glass Votive Holder

You can easily make attractive candle votives by covering glass with translucent polymer clays. This votive is inspired by Tiffany glass lamps and uses nothing more than an ordinary, large wine glass for its base. Mix a little colored clay into the translucent to make the custom colors used in this project or use the pre-colored translucent clays available. The quantities below are enough to cover a large glass, you may wish to adjust the amount to suit whatever size you use.

Skill level
✳ ✳ ✳

You will need

* ½ block blue-colored translucent polymer clay
* ½ block yellow-colored translucent polymer clay
* ½ block fuchsia-colored translucent polymer clay
* ⅛ block purple polymer clay
* ⅛ block blue polymer clay
* 1 block scrap polymer clay

* Clay gun (optional)
* Craft knife
* Tissue blade
* 1 large wine glass
* Pasta machine or hand roller
* Wet/dry sandpaper in 600 and 1200 grit
* PVA glue
* Silver-colored bronze or mica powder or silver acrylic paint
* Paintbrush and varnish

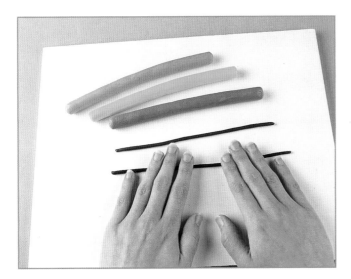

1 Form the colored translucent clays into logs approximately 15 mm (⅝ in) diameter. Roll the purple and blue clay into 3 mm (⅛ in) diameter strings, the same length as the logs. The logs and strings do not need to be evenly rolled; the effect will be enhanced by having some irregularities so do not worry about making them perfect.

2 Attach the blue string to the blue translucent log. Lay the string along the length of the log, pushing it gently on to the top to adhere. Repeat the process attaching the purple string to the top of the fuchsia translucent log.

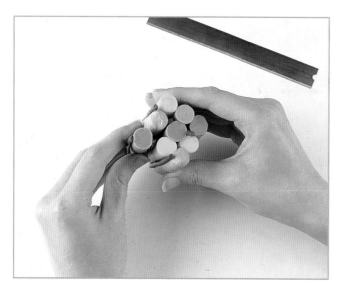

3 Cut each log into three equal sections. Stack all the sections together to form a simple square shaped mosaic cane. Ensure that every layer and row of the cane has a section of each color, with no log placed next to another of the same color.

4 Reduce the cane until you have a square-shaped cane 15 mm (⅝ in) across. There is no need to let the cane rest before reducing; it does not matter if the cane distorts as it gets thinner. Cut the reduced cane into four equal sections and combine these together to form a larger square cane. Squeeze the cane together well to ensure air is forced out but do not reduce any further.

5 Cut 2 mm (³⁄₃₂ in) slices from the cane. Lay the slices to form a sheet, butting the edges together so they adhere. Make the sheet as wide as the height of the bowl of the wine glass. Make the length of the sheet approximately two thirds of the circumference of the glass at its widest point.

6 Fold the sheet in half and roll to approximately 3 mm (⅛ in) thick. Always roll lengthways along the sheet if rolling by hand. You can use a pasta machine to roll the clay, providing your sheet is no wider than the pasta machine's rollers.

7 Fold the sheet in half once more and this time roll to a thickness of 1 mm (1/32 in). This will blend and overlap the colors slightly giving striations imitating streaky colored glass. Hold the sheet to the light to check the effect of the translucent clay, if you want a more blended effect you can fold and roll the sheet one more time.

8 Wrap the sheet around the bowl of the glass, trimming away the excess. Smooth the clay on to the glass, working from the middle outwards. At the top, smooth the clay over the edge and into the glass. As you smooth the clay towards the stem it may be necessary to remove small sections from the sheet. If the clay starts to pucker, cut away the surplus clay and smooth the seams together neatly.

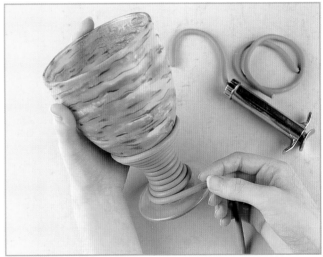

9 Continue smoothing the clay until no air bubbles remain. You can slice stubborn bubbles open with the craft knife to expel the air, smoothing the clay over afterwards. Trim around the inside edge of the glass with a craft knife and cut a neat line around the stem. Bake according to the clay manufacturer's instructions then allow to cool slowly. When cool, wet-sand the clay smooth.

10 Coat the stem and base of the glass with PVA glue and let it dry. Roll a long log of scrap clay 5 mm (3/16 in) in diameter. Use a clay gun or roll by hand. Wind the log around the stem and base of the glass, starting from just above the top of the stem. If you use more than one log, cut a neat edge at the end of the log and continue with a new one, keeping the seams on the same side of the glass.

11 Apply silver-colored bronze or mica powder to the scrap clay using a soft brush. When all the clay is covered bake again according to the clay manufacturer's instructions and allow to cool slowly. As an alternative to using powders, the clay base can be painted with silver acrylic paint. Bake the votive holder first and when cool give the base two coats of paint. Varnish the votive to protect the metallic finish on the base and also make the colors on the bowl more vibrant when the votive is unlit.

Variation: **Small Votive Holder**

All shapes and sizes of glass can be used to make polymer clay votives. This small wine glass has a fretwork detail around the top of the stem of the glass. It was made by extruding scrap polymer clay from a clay gun using a clover-shaped die.

Safety

Always wear a protective face mask when using decorative powders.

Never leave the votive unattended when lit.

Suppliers and Useful Addresses

United Kingdom

Craft Creations Ltd
Ingersoll House
Dalamare Road
Cheshunt
Hertfordshire
EN8 9HD
Tel: 01992 781 900
Email: enquiries@craftcreations.com
www.craftcreations.com
For greetings cards blanks

EJR Beads
81 Woodcote Grove Road
Coulsdon, Surrey
CR5 2AL
Email: info@ejrbeads.co.uk
www.ejrbeads.co.uk
*For wine glass charmer blanks,
silver beads and wooden printing
blocks as used in various projects.*

Fred Aldous Ltd
37 Lever Street
Manchester
M1 1LW
Tel: 08707 517 300
Email: aldous@btinternet.com
www.fredaldous.co.uk
Craft supplies and tools

OPITEC Hobbyfix
Unit 51, Basepoint Centre
Anderson's Road
Southampton
SO14 5FE
Tel: 023 8068 2401
Email: info.uk@opitec.com
www.uk.opitec.com
*Craft supplies, including the
aluminium sheet as used in the
Clay and Metal Earrings project.*

Oasis Art & Craft Products
Goldthorn Road, Kidderminster
Worcestershire
DY11 7JN
Tel: 01562 744 522
*Distributor for Sculpey III and other
Polyform products. Contact to find
a retailer in your area.*

The Polymer Clay Pit
16 Millers Drive, Dickleburgh
Diss, Norfolk IP21 4PX
Tel: 01379 742 789
Email : sue@claypit.fslife.co.uk
www.polymerclaypit.co.uk
*Retailer for Premo!, Sculpey and
other polymer clay tools, books
and videos, with a link to the*
British Polymer Clay Guild

Specialist Crafts Ltd
PO Box 247
Leicester LE1 9QS
Tel: 0116 269 7711
Email: post@speccrafts.co.uk
www.speccrafts.co.uk
Craft supplies and tools

Staedtler (UK) Ltd
Pontyclun, Mid Glamorgan
Wales CF72 8YJ
Tel: 01443 237 421
Email:enquiries@uk.staedtler.com
*Distributor for Fimo Classic, Fimo
Soft and Easy Metal imitation
metal leaf. Contact to find a
retailer in your area.*

Europe

Eberhard Faber GmbH
Postfach 1220
D- 92302 Neumarkt
Germany
Tel: 09181 430 0
Fimo Classic, Fimo Soft, Easy Metal

T&F Kunstoffe GmbH
Postfach 301236
D-63274 Dreieich
Germany
Cernit

USA

**National Polymer Clay Guild
(USA)**
www.npcg.org
*Information on the national guild
and listings of regional guilds
throughout the United States*

**Polyform Products
Company, Inc**
1901 Estes Avenue
Elk Grove Village
IL 60007
*Premo!, Sculpey, Sculpey III,
Translucent Liquid Sculpey*

**Polymer Clay Express at
TheArtWay Studio**
13017 Wisteria Drive
Box 275
Germantown
MD 20874
Tel: 301 482 0435
www.polymerclayexpress.com

**Rupert, Gibbon
& Spider, Inc.**
P.O. Box 425
Healdsbury
CA 95448
Toll free: 800 442 0455
Tel: 707-433-9577
service@jacquardproducts.com
*Manufacturers of Jacquard Pearl-Ex
Pigment powders, Pinata Colors,
Lumiere and Neopaque paints.*

Australia

**Cam Art, Science &
Technology**
197 Blackburn Rd
Mount Waverley
Victoria 3149
03 9802 4200
www.camartech.com.au

Modelene
www.modelene.com.au

New Zealand

**Zigzag Polymer Clay
Supplies Ltd**
8 Cherry Place
Casebrook
Christchurch 8005
Tel: 03 359 2989
Email: sales@zigzag.co.nz
www.zigzag.co.nz

Gordon Harris Art Supplies
4 Gillies Avenue
Newmarket
Tel: 09 520 4466
and
31 Symonds Street
Auckland Central
Tel: 09 377 9992
Email:
artsupplies@gordonharris.co.nz

Studio Art Supplies
81 Parnell Rise
Parnell
Auckland
Tel: 09 377 0302
Email: studio.art@xtra.co.nz

The French Art Shop
33 Ponsonby Road
Ponsonby
Tel: 09 376 0610

Littlejohns
170 Victoria Street
Wellington
Tel: 04 385 2099
Email: Littlejohns@xtra.co.nz

Spotlight Stores
Locations throughout New
Zealand:
Whangarei 09 430 7220
Wairau Park 09 444 0220
Henderson 09 836 0888
Pamure 09 527 0915
Manukau 09 263 6760
Hamilton 07 839 1793
Rotorua 07 343 6901
New Plymouth 06 757 3575
Hastings 06 878 5223
Palmerston North 06 357 6833
Porirua 04 237 0650
Wellington 04 472 5600
Christchurch 03 377 6121
Dunedin 03 477 1478
www.spotlight.net.nz
*Wide range of craft and decorative
painting supplies*

Index